# Herding Professional Cats

Being advice to aspiring leaders in the professions

*Graeme Davies and Geoff Garrett*

First published in 2013 by:
Triarchy Press
Station Offices
Axminster
Devon. EX13 5PF
United Kingdom

+44 (0)1297 631456
info@triarchypress.net
www.triarchypress.net

© Graeme Davies and Geoff Garrett, 2013.

The right of Graeme Davies and Geoff Garrett to be identified as the authors of this book has been asserted by them in accordance with the Copyright, Designs and Patents Act, 1988.

All rights reserved.

No part of this publication may be reproduced, stored in a retrieval system or transmitted in any form or by any means including photocopying, electronic, mechanical, recording or otherwise, without the prior written permission of the publisher.

A catalogue record for this book is available from the British Library.

Cover artwork by Walter Pichler

Print ISBN: 978-1-909470-20-0
EPub ISBN: 978-1-909470-21-7

www.triarchypress.net/prof-cats

**Triarchy Press** is an independent publishing house that looks at how organisations work and how to make them work better. We present challenging perspectives on organisations in short and pithy, but rigorously argued, books.

For more information about Triarchy Press, or to order any of our publications, please visit our website or drop us a line:

www.triarchypress.net

We're on Twitter: @TriarchyPress
and Facebook: www.facebook.com/triarchypress

# Cats will not be commanded and can choose their owner

Valeria Manferto De Fabianis (ed.)
*Cats*
(White Star Publishers, 2007)

Once again for Florence and Janet –
caring and staunch supporters throughout all our
professional ups and downs

## CONTENTS

| | |
|---|---|
| AUTHORS' FOREWORD | 7 |
| ACKNOWLEDGEMENTS | 9 |
| HOW TO USE THIS BOOK | 15 |
| HOW THE BOOK WORKS | 17 |
| INTRODUCTION | 19 |
| **A: UNDERSTANDING THE CULTURE** | **21** |
|     1. Aspects of the CULTURE | 22 |
|     2. On CONFLICT | 29 |
|     3. The difficulty of COLLABORATION and boundary crossing | 33 |
| **B: GETTING THE JOB DONE** | **39** |
|     4. Taking CHARGE | 39 |
|     5. COMPOSURE under pressure and the implementation imperative | 60 |
|     6. COMMITTEES and meetings | 68 |
|     7. Managing the CASH | 76 |
| **C: MANAGING THE PEOPLE** | **82** |
|     8. COLLEAGUES not subordinates ("It's all about the people") | 82 |
|     9. COMMUNICATION, COMMUNICATION, COMMUNICATION | 103 |
|     10. Giving CREDIT | 115 |
| **D: LEADING STRATEGICALLY** | **121** |
|     11. Strategy is about CHOICE | 121 |
|     12. Leading and managing CHANGE | 130 |
| POSTSCRIPT – A CLOSING THOUGHT | 139 |
| ABOUT THE AUTHORS | 142 |
| INDEX | 145 |

## AUTHORS' FOREWORD

Over much of the forty years we have known each other, we have enjoyed trading 'war stories' around what we have learned, and observed, about the business of managing/ leading academic and research institutions – effectively, and otherwise. As a consequence, some years back we committed to the discipline of putting pen to paper and created a small 'guidebook' for aspiring (and practising) leaders in our work-world. This was published in late 2010 and went to reprint early in 2011. One of the reviewers, Mark Dodgson in the Australian Literary Review, said about it:

> "*Herding Cats* sets out to share the considerable experience of its authors in managing researchers, but its consequence is much more widespread. It really confronts the challenge of managing intelligent, opinionated, independent and frequently difficult people or, in other words, professionals. This is of interest to professionals themselves – lawyers, doctors, consultants, accountants, journalists; knowledge workers, in the contemporary parlance, and those who manage them."

This – and other feedback we received – prompted us to revisit our original manuscript and adapt it for the 'professionals'. So in offering advice, somewhat tentatively, around leading and 'managing' professionals, the well-known idea of 'herding cats' seemed to us again to be an appropriate metaphor.

As a central part of the process of creating the original book, we recognised that it would be extremely valuable to tap into the wisdom and experience of a number of the senior academic and research leaders around the world with whom we had interacted over the years, and whom we admired. From their responses, coupled with our own perspectives, we realised that we might pull together some 'key lessons' that could be worth recording, and sharing. For this book we have repeated this process with leaders from other professional spheres –

accountants, lawyers, architects, engineers, as well as medical administrators, media bosses, public servants and politicians – located in various parts of the world, seeking their comments.

To this end we again posed a series of questions, along the lines of...

- What do you know now that you wish you had known 'back then' – when you commenced – or got immersed in – your leadership career?
- If you are mentoring a new leader – a head of an operating department, a programme manager – what would you wish to share, concisely, about 'operations'?... about 'strategy'?
- What are your favourite 'war stories'? – providing lessons that we might share with our prospective audience – about 'herding professional cats'?
- What, in your opinion, brings out the best (and worst) in your people?

In compiling this new edition, we have found that many of the comments we received from the senior academic and research leaders whom we had originally consulted were generic in nature, and as such (in our view) were more generally applicable. So when going through them for inclusion in *Herding Professional Cats* we exercised some editorial license and, with the contributors' approval, have adapted some of these quotations, in order to relate them to the wider professional domains – without altering the sense of the original comments.

We have also added some new sections. For instance, those relating to Social Media, Work-Life Balance and Governance and Ethics.

This modest second volume is what has resulted.

## ACKNOWLEDGEMENTS

There's an old Chinese saying: 'An evening across the table with a wise man is worth a month of study in books'. We have had the good fortune of many such interactions over the years – perhaps not always a full evening (or even a dinner), but quality time in conversation with wise and informed men and women. Their ideas and experiences have helped forge our own thinking, and are greatly appreciated.

We hope our distillation of their thoughts, and our own, will merit your study.

We are especially indebted to the following people for helping us in our original quest and in our follow-up venture. Their various contributions, non-attributed, appear (in indented italics) throughout our text.

**Joan Adams** – formerly Vice President, Battelle, USA
**Rich Adams** – formerly Senior Vice President, Battelle, USA
**Stephen Akers** – Consultant, Mollis, Switzerland
**Karin Alexander** – Web Index Manager, World Wide Web Foundation
**Bridget Allchin** – formerly of Wolfson College, Cambridge, UK
**Sheridan Ash** – Director, PricewaterhouseCoopers LLP, UK
**Bai Chunli** – President, Chinese Academy of Sciences, Beijing, China
**Michael Barber** – Vice-Chancellor, Flinders University, Australia
**Michael Battaglia** – Theme Leader, CSIRO, Australia
**Robin Batterham** – Kernot Professor of Engineering, Melbourne University; formerly Chief Technologist of Rio Tinto and Chief Scientist of Australia
**Attila Brungs** – Deputy Vice-Chancellor (Research), University of Technology, Sydney, Australia

**Curtis Carlson** – Chief Executive, SRI International, Menlo Park, USA

**Ian Chubb** – Chief Scientist, Government of Australia; formerly Vice-Chancellor, Australian National University, Australia

**Geoffrey Crossick** – formerly Warden, Goldsmiths, University of London, UK and Vice-Chancellor, University of London, UK

**Simon Davies** – Firmwide Managing Partner, Linklaters LLP

**Glyn Davis** – Vice-Chancellor, University of Melbourne, Australia

**Ian Dean** – Leadership consultant, Stellenbosch, South Africa

**Mark Dodgson** – Director, Technology and Innovation Management Centre, School of Business, University of Queensland, Australia

**Annie Duncan** – Chairman, Australian Communities Foundation; formerly Chief Executive, Questacon, Australia

**Peter Duncan** – Chairman, Orica Ltd; formerly Chief Executive, Shell Australia

**David Eastwood** – Vice-Chancellor, Birmingham University, UK

**Andrew Einhorn** – Founder and CEO, Numeric NPC, Cape Town, South Africa

**Charles Elachi** – Director, Jet Propulsion Laboratory, USA

**Boel Flodgren** – Professor of Law, and former President of Lund University, Sweden

**Margaret Gardner** – Vice-Chancellor, RMIT University, Australia

**Geoffrey Green** – formerly Senior Partner, Ashurst LLP, UK

**John Greene** – University of Cape Town, South Africa

**Julia Goodfellow** – Vice-Chancellor, University of Kent, UK

**Paul Greenfield** – formerly Vice-Chancellor, University of Queensland, Australia

**Peter Høj** – Vice-Chancellor, University of Queensland, Australia

**Graham Humphries** – Senior Partner, Cox Rayner Architects, Canberra, Australia

**Richard Larkins** – formerly Vice-Chancellor, Monash University, Australia

**Debbie Lawrence** – Operations Manager, Thompson Reuters, London

**Erkki Leppavuori** – President and CEO, VTT Technical Research Centre, Finland

**Ramesh Mashelkar** – President, Global Research Alliance; formerly Director General, CSIR National Laboratories, India

**Keith McNeil** – Chief Executive, Cambridge University Hospitals NHS Foundation Trust, UK

**Clive Mattieson** – Editor, *The Australian*, Sydney, Australia

**Graham Mitchell** – Chief Executive, Foursight Associates, Australia

**Geraldine Chin Moody** – formerly Chief Operating Officer, Baker & McKenzie, Sydney, Australia

**David Morley** – Senior Partner, Allen & Overy LLP, UK

**Robert Morris** – Vice President, Global Labs, IBM Research, Shanghai, China

**Gus Nossal** – formerly Director, Walter and Eliza Hall Institute, Melbourne, Australia

**Jim Peacock** – CSIRO; formerly Chief Scientist, Government of Australia

**David Penington** – formerly Vice-Chancellor, University of Melbourne, Australia

**Ian Powell** – Senior Partner, PriceWaterhouseCoopers LLP, UK

**Max Price** – Vice-Chancellor, University of Cape Town, South Africa

**Alan Robson** – formerly Vice-Chancellor, University of Western Australia

**Craig Roy** – Deputy Chief Executive, CSIRO, Australia

**Louise Ryan** – formerly Chief, Mathematical and Information Sciences, CSIRO, Australia, and Professor of Biostatistics, Harvard University, USA

**Ron Sandland** – formerly Deputy Chief Executive, CSIRO, Australia

**Richard Sexton** – Executive Board member, PriceWaterhouseCoopers LLP, UK

**Bernard Shapiro** – formerly Principal, McGill University, Canada

**Vince Sharma** – Partner, Norton Rose Pty Ltd, Canberra, Australia

**Margaret Sheil** – ProVice-Chancellor, University of Melbourne; formerly Chief Executive, Australian Research Council, Australia

**Peter Shergold** – Chancellor, University of Western Sydney; formerly Head of the Australian Public Service

**Fiona Simpson, MP** – Speaker of the Queensland Parliament, Brisbane, Australia

**Adrian Smith** – Vice-Chancellor, University of London; formerly Director General for Science and Research, Department for Business, Innovation and Skills, UK

**George Smith** – Emeritus Professor of Materials Science, University of Oxford, UK

**Mark Stafford-Smith** – Science Director, Climate Adaptation Flagship, CSIRO; formerly CEO, Desert Knowledge Cooperative Research Centre, Australia

**Ian Steadman** – Director of Development, Oxford Brookes University, UK

**John Stuckey** – former Managing Partner, McKinsey & Company, Australia

**Mandy Thomas** – formerly Pro Vice-Chancellor, Australian National University, Australia

**Rick Trainor** – Principal, King's College London, UK

**Jeff Wadsworth** – President and CEO, Battelle, USA

**David Watson** – Master, Green Templeton College, Oxford; formerly Vice-Chancellor, University of Brighton, UK

**Paul Wellings** – Vice-Chancellor, University of Wollongong, Australia; formerly Vice-Chancellor, University of Lancaster, UK

**Bert Westwood** – formerly Corporate Vice President of Research and Technology, Lockheed Martin Corporation, USA

**David Williams** – Dean, College of Engineering, Ohio State University; formerly President, University of Alabama in Huntsville, USA

**John Wood** – Secretary-General, Association of Commonwealth Universities, London; formerly Chief Executive of the Central Laboratories of the Research Councils, UK

**Alex Zelinsky** – Chief Executive, Defence Science and Technology Organisation, Australia

We are particularly indebted on this occasion to Karin Alexander, Sheridan Ash, Mark Dodgson and Geoffrey Green, and, with the original book, to Ian Dean, David Williams and John Wood, who generously gave of their time, not only to share their insights, but also as 'key readers' of the manuscript, offering numerous helpful suggestions.

Two texts, in particular, provided us with our original inspiration – in very different ways, indeed 'chalk and cheese' some might say: Francis Cornford's *Microcosmographia Academica*, which first appeared in 1908, and from which we have borrowed the sentiment for our sub-title; and Robert Townsend's *Up the Organisation* (1970) which provided a helpful, alphabetical 'taxonomy' for arranging the substantial feedback we received. These two volumes, written six decades apart, are also direct and to the point, a practice which we have tried to follow in our own text.

We are also grateful to Sean Davies of Amrop Cordiner King, Melbourne, for supplying copies of their excellent career booklets, *Taking Charge* and *Maintaining the Balance*, which provided us with a guide to the useful consultation and quotation approach we have employed, we hope with positive effect.

Special thanks are due to Biddy Greene of Cape Town for editorial support – without her eagle-eyed professionalism and her cheerful, constructive input we would have had a much less polished manuscript. Also to all of the team at our publishers, Triarchy Press, but especially to Imogen Charnley for her enthusiasm, advice and commitment.

We would once again like to acknowledge, with thanks, the encouragement and learning opportunities provided, over many years, by our respective institutions, and by our splendid colleagues therein.

Finally, we wish you well in your own 'cat-herding' adventures and would be very pleased to hear about your own experiences: graeme.davies@london.ac.uk; geoff.g.garrett@gmail.com

GD and GG
London and Brisbane
April 2013

## HOW TO USE THIS BOOK

Read it.

In any order.

Maybe with a pencil in your hand – which you should **USE**.

If you thought it was helpful, read it again in six months' time.

Perhaps with a different-coloured pencil.

And if you just want to dip in, then the **INDEX** might help.

## HOW THE BOOK WORKS

As you might have skipped the Foreword, Introduction and so on, here, before you begin, is a labelled example to show you how we've constructed this book.

*This is the main text – by us, the authors.*

In most knowledge-worker based organisations, for better or for worse, the culture at any particular time is frequently determined by the immediate past, as well as being influenced, to a greater or lesser extent, by the more distant past.

> *Clear thinking about the history, nature and direction, and development of your particular organisation or group… is imperative. The past lives on in most organisations, influencing attitudes and judgements in a manner which is often deeply hidden. Successfully managing change depends on getting these issues out into the open.*

*The bits in indented italics like this are words of wisdom gleaned from our colleagues and friends. As well as giving sage advice, they show you that YOU ARE NOT ALONE!*

But then there's this:

> "The further backward you can look, the further forward you can see." Winston Churchill (1874–1965).

*Words indented and in quote marks are quotations from 'famous people' that we couldn't resist adding.*

Established professionals are usually clever people, and clever people normally function in ways quite different from others. They can revel in – indeed even exploit – the complex.

*Us again. Telling you what we think…*

\* \* \* \*

Each of the four parts A through D – which package the 'key topics' of our twelve sections – commences with some introductory scene-setting, and concludes with an executive summary labelled 'In Conclusion'.

At the end of the book, our Postscript attempts to encapsulate, in a page or so, the essence of what we address in the text, and our Index – which provides ready access to details of the topics – may be useful for reference purposes.

# INTRODUCTION

Professional partnerships and businesses, like academic and research institutions, have one critically important common characteristic when it comes to considering how they might best be led and managed. All are staffed by women and men of high intellectual ability who pride themselves on their skill at thinking and acting creatively, and independently. There is usually no culture of uniformity. 'Command and control' approaches do not prosper; timescales, to get things done, may at times be lengthy; disagreement, ubiquitous.

This means that the staff of these professional partnerships and businesses can require a set of leadership and management skills somewhat different from (but, of course, with many parallels to) those often considered more characteristic of the 'command and control' world of commerce and industry. The 'carrot' will certainly predominate over the 'stick', and the carrots will vary.

There is a place for guile and political acumen.

It is this that leads to the metaphor of 'herding cats' – if you have to try to coordinate a very difficult situation, where people want to do very different things, you're herding cats.

Our aim in this slim volume is to show that the trick with 'cats' (and by that we mean with practising professionals) is to know that it is a lot harder to push them to a destination than it is to tempt them to an outcome.

That is, of course, what makes managing them so challenging. And so rewarding.

\* \* \*

In bringing together our thoughts, and the thoughts of others, we have sought, in the way we have organised the material, to follow the sort of timeline that a new leader and manager is likely to face on taking up a new post, or a promotion. Of course, these do not form a simple sequence since there will necessarily be much overlap.

We believe that good leaders and managers must be able to deal with these matters both in parallel and in sequence.

Thus there is, first, the need to understand the cultural climate in which the new leader's (often multiple) roles are carried out. Then, attention must be given to mastering the priorities of getting on with the new job. As one's skills and experience build, the need to be on top of the people- management issues becomes paramount. Lastly, for the longer term, formulating strategy and implementing change take precedence.

\* \* \*

Finally, in addition to the obvious (and somewhat fortuitous, and only marginally forced) Cat linkages – the 'twelve Cs' of our Contents emerged from our jointly seeking to identify, and summarise for ourselves, key learnings from our own deliberations and consultations. They merely provide advice, and are certainly not 'Commandments'!

We trust that they will provide a useful aide-memoire for those in the professions aspiring to be leaders, or to be better leaders.

## A: UNDERSTANDING THE CULTURE

According to conventional wisdom, 'Culture' has a significant influence on all dimensions of organisational life. It is often described as 'the way we do things around here'.

While there are obvious differences between the various professions – whether we're talking about lawyers, accountants, architects, academics, public servants or politicians – that are largely associated with differing missions and outcomes, their cultural dimensions are surprisingly similar in being notoriously complex.

In seeking to provide guidance to aspiring (and practising) leaders in the professional environment – often referred to as a 'knowledge worker' environment – we have chosen in the sections that follow to address cultural issues that we, and the majority of the colleagues we consulted, believe are ripe, and indeed the priority, for reflection. These include:

- the relatively conservative nature of the culture forged, and still often influenced, by history;
- the high IQ of the workforce;
- their correspondingly high ideals but commonly challenging style;
- the often bureaucratic nature of many institutional processes and 'administrations';
- the immense difficulties, and huge advantages, in seeking cross-boundary collaboration;
- the nature of conflict – political, emotional, historical – and suggestions for its effective resolution (or at least understanding) in a 'cats' environment.

## 1. Aspects of the CULTURE

In the Introduction we made the point that different professions generally have cultures of their own. Accepting this, and then gaining an understanding of these differing cultures, is critical to leading and managing in these professions.

> *It is difficult to underestimate the differences of culture in the wide range of activities embraced by the word 'business'. These cannot all be resolved, so it is necessary to reinforce the conviction that being part of the bigger team is the thing you have in common.*

We first consider some background issues, central – in our view – to developing an understanding of culture in the professional environment. We then go on to explore a range of other issues, many of which embrace concepts involving change. In our concluding section (Section 12), we return to address further issues and approaches for leading sustainable change.

**Cats will not be commanded...** This fact – that cats are generally unwilling to be instructed – requires the cat-herder's understanding of just what leadership demands in this environment.

> *Professionals like to lead but they do not like being led. I often felt more like a gardener – watering a little here, weeding a little there, trying to cross-fertilize or simply trying to make things grow where the long shadows from some of the 'giant trees' sometimes made it difficult for anything to grow.*

> *You cannot, in our sort of organisation, order people about.*

You can, of course, but it won't get you very far, even in the short term.

> *One of my colleagues was senior in the Army before he joined our ranks. He remarked, "In the Army we used to argue like mad, but when the decision was made, that was it. A hundred per cent alignment, and a focus on action, and getting the job done. In this place, when the decision*

A: UNDERSTANDING THE CULTURE

*is made it seems to signal the starting gun for the debate to commence in earnest, using all the 'political' weapons at peoples' disposal!"*

*Our folk do not generally respond well to managerialism or rules or instructions.*

*Coming from industry, I found the culture in this specialist organisation so very different... primarily around the need for autonomy, and with success measured by individual credibility and individual performance... 'top-down' doesn't work in our type of organisation.*

*There is a real difference when you're having to get everything done through influence as opposed to through authority.*

## Learning from history...

"Those who cannot remember the past are condemned to repeat it." George Santayana (1863–1952)

In most knowledge-worker based organisations, for better or for worse, the culture at any particular time is frequently determined by the immediate past, as well as being influenced, to a greater or lesser extent, by the more distant past. Thus:

*Clear thinking about the history, nature and direction, and development of your particular organisation or group... is imperative. The past lives on in most organisations, influencing attitudes and judgements in a manner which is often deeply hidden. Successfully managing change depends on getting these issues out into the open.*

This recognition of the influence of the past may explain to some extent the view that...

*With our organisation having been around for so very many years, there is a very special culture here, nourished by a strong self esteem and a feeling of being a very important institution in society, but, at the same time, we have a very inward-looking culture. The long history – which is*

> *something that usually counts in our work world – adds to the prestige… and makes it difficult for the leader to try to 'modernise'.*
>
> *Historically, different professions have developed some quite different cultures – the same thinking and approach usually doesn't work across the board.*

Understanding the cultural 'landscape', and its history, may help clarify a considerable range of situations and make them more understandable. And help you craft your future strategy:

> "The further backward you can look, the further forward you can see." Winston Churchill (1874–1965)

**Why are we here?…** Established professionals are usually clever people, and clever people normally function in ways quite different from others. They can revel in – indeed even exploit – the complex. Thus, in stark contrast to the old adage about genius being the art of making the complex seem simple…

> *Many experts want to wrap their subject up and make it seem very difficult, and far beyond a normal person's understanding, thus showing that they're very clever. It can be all about preserving a mystique.*
>
> *Our folks have always been the smartest people in the room and they want to keep it that way.*

They can also revel in the minutiae…

> *It's amazing how so many very clever people just focus on the detail and then only the detail that applies to them. And frequently very trivial detail at that.*

Nevertheless, it is important to recognise that…

> *Here, above all, people are looking for profile, and respect – from the community, their peers and their bosses.*

> *Mostly our people are motivated to help shape how, through their guidance, the next generation sees the world; or how, through their innovation, they can actually change the world.*
>
> *People look to a career in the professions because they want to achieve. It is their core identity.*

In addition, certain core values are intrinsic and ubiquitous – most particularly, the pursuit of excellence and the recognition of the importance of fairness and equity.

**The political bias...**

> *I wish I had known earlier that I needed to think more politically and not only down the 'straight and narrow' disciplinary path.*

Notwithstanding the need to be persuasive, it is essential to recognise that bias may also require appeals (of varying strength) to prejudice and to political motivations. For example, it was said with regard to the academic profession that...

> "The Political Motive in the academic breast is honest enough – it is Fear – genuine, perpetual, heartfelt timorousness... and the proper objects of Fear are, in order of importance: giving yourself away; females; what will Dr ... say?; and the public washing of [dirty] linen... This is the central mystery of academic politics." Francis Cornford (1874–1943)

**Talking straight...** This can be a real dilemma. Being open, transparent and honest inevitably will imply communicating some bad news. Correctly managed, straight talk can establish a 'burning platform' motivation for change. Badly handled, it can provide a cause célèbre and an opportunity for your opponents to use every available channel (media, politicians, government bureaucrats, your staff) to communicate that, actually, it is you who are the problem.

> *When I arrived I assumed I could speak straight, and tell them how I saw it. And I did. I soon learned, regrettably, that I had to speak more like a politician – congratulate the questioner on his intelligent observations; not answer the question directly; answer the question with a question; etc, etc. It is a sadness. If I disagreed with people it was not a professional argument, I was being authoritative.*

But at times this 'solution' may not be wholly appropriate:

> *If you've got bad news, you'd better front up. Pretending is a bad idea.*

> *Honesty is always respected, even if it causes a stir – sometimes it's good to create a stir – that is, not always to be a 'politician'.*

So, while we feel that straightness has definite virtues, all good leaders will need to develop the ability to judge how differing approaches need to be balanced and when it may be prudent to exercise a little restraint in confronting colleagues.

**Bureaucracy rules, OK?...** It can be convenient to blame many problems and issues on the bureaucratic nature of the organisation. However...

> *The biggest thing that I have found out through the years is that many professional people are actually bureaucrats at heart. I would have expected them all to be interested in the future, wanting to change the world, brimming over with enthusiasm to get on with the job and deliver useful results. This took me a long time to realise and I think I would have been much more effective if I had understood that there are a lot of people who really do not want to see much in the way of change.*

Consider this sentiment within the definition (from Chambers' Dictionary): **bureaucracy** (*noun*)... any system of administration in which matters are hindered by excessive adherence to minor rules and procedures.

And we know that, left unattended, bureaucracies can tend to bloat, recognising that – as Cyril Northcote Parkinson (of Parkinson's Law fame) observed:

> "There need be little or no relationship between the work to be done and the size of the staff to which it may be assigned."

Noting also…

> "Rational bureaucrats… will always and everywhere seek to increase their budgets in order to increase their own power." William A. Niskanen (1933–2011), American economist, and Chairman of the Cato Institute.

For these reasons bureaucracy can be anathema to many of our colleagues. Nevertheless, we recognise that there is inherent bureaucracy in many professional organisations, as encapsulated in this viewpoint:

*Coming into this place, I was amazed how extraordinarily rules-based we are.*

In quite a lot of 'clever' organisations, this perspective does not seem to have changed much over the last hundred years:

> "(One) must never be troubled with having to think whether this or that ought to be done or not; it should be settled by rules. Plainly, the more rules you can invent, the less need there will be to waste time over fruitless puzzling about right and wrong." Francis Cornford (1874–1943)

The trouble with this, of course, is that…

*Unnecessary, unexplained red tape is a killer of morale.*

Most particularly, in a difficult financial environment bureaucracy can flourish:

> *When the budgets got tough, the bureaucrats got into high gear: a junior colleague remarked "sometimes it feels like we have difficulty in getting a chair moved around here!*

Vigilance is needed – in good financial times as well as bad – for excessive red tape to be avoided. This can pay real motivational dividends:

> *The active minimisation of unnecessary red tape and good explanations around why some bureaucratic processes are necessary, if they cannot be avoided, scores high 'brownie points' in the motivation business.*

Notice that this says 'good explanations', not just 'explanations'. This notion can be made more explicit:

> *Good leaders give a sense of being 'on the side' of their colleagues (and of common sense), seeking a way around bureaucratic obstacles rather than hiding behind them.*

And there is light at the end of the tunnel:

> *Most professionals will be persuaded by reason and, by and large, are driven by the same altruistic intent that has driven them to a life in the professions. Thus, if the guiding principle is 'to achieve excellence in professional achievement', and the argument can be made that, given the prevailing constraints – for example the need for financial responsibility and viability, efficient management to avoid chaos, accountability to meet the requirement of Government, stakeholders and the general community, etc. – if all your actions and those you are wishing your staff to pursue are in the ultimate interests of the excellence you seek, then by and large colleagues will seek to do what you would like them to do.*

But this must be seen in an overall context:

> *The support framework you develop must be high quality and efficient so as to leave your cats doing what they do best.*

## 2. On CONFLICT

*'Cats' come with extraordinary talent and abilities; but on the counter side, they often come with major issues and you get left picking up the pieces.*

**Funny places...** By their very nature, many professional organisations can be somewhat strange environments. They can be worlds of their own. This reflects both the characteristics of the staff and the nature of their pursuits.

*Most of my colleagues are professionally questioning and indeed somewhat argumentative – more or less everybody is authorised to have an opinion about everything! And issues tend to generate heat in inverse proportion to their importance.*

This can manifest itself in conflicts of varying degrees of intensity. Conflict may be hard, at first, to identify. For example:

*The first thing said in a discussion may well be the exact opposite of what the speaker means. "I'd like to agree with everything the Chairman has just said, but..." or "With respect..." (often meaning quite the opposite).*

It is also often extraordinary how myopic and bloody-minded some very intelligent people can be when issues are outside their comfort zone, or (especially) when issues – such as remuneration – appear to affect their comfort zone in an adverse way.

*In many situations, whatever your decision or the collective decision, you will always upset one group or another. Even doing nothing will upset some people.*

*No decision you ever make will receive universal support. Abolishing the difference in car parking rights between the professional and the support staff led to the greatest criticism of any decision I made.*

Thus, people who in their 'normal' professional lives commission research and weigh up evidence, and draw (mostly) sensible conclusions, become suspicious, spurn a logical argument out of hand or provide forty-seven – often mostly spurious – reasons why 'it' can't, or shouldn't, be done: "There's no way I can move offices in July; I have proposals to write."

**Peer pressure...** In seeking to resolve conflict, sensible peer pressure, carefully harnessed, can be helpful and facilitate the effective management of change:

> *If the well-respected Mary or Fred down the corridor says "That's a good idea", hitherto illogically-argued resistance around 'issues of principle' may suddenly fall away.*

**Techniques of opposition, and resistance...** You will perhaps have noticed by now that Francis Cornford's name crops up regularly. Cornford (1874–1943) was an English classical scholar and poet, and a Fellow of Trinity College, Cambridge. Written just over a century ago, his excellent little book *Microcosmographia Academica, Being a Guide for the Young Academic Politician*, focuses on the political realities and intrigues of academic life and, as we mentioned in our acknowledgements, we have found it remarkably pertinent to our endeavour. We believe it could usefully be required reading for leaders/managers in the professions, as well as those in academia. Many of Cornford's observations, while geared towards the university establishment, do seem quite applicable to many other professional occupations, and remain as alive and well today as they were more than a hundred years ago:

> "The Principle of the Dangerous Precedent is that you should not now do an admittedly right action for fear you, or your equally timid successors, should not have the courage to do right in some future case."

> "The Fair Trial argument – 'give the present system a fair trial'… is especially useful in withstanding changes."
>
> "The alternative proposal [is] an accepted means of obstruction… as soon as three or more alternatives are in the field, there is pretty sure to be a majority against any one of them, and nothing will be done."
>
> "The Last Ditch [is] a place which you may safely threaten to die… If you did die, nobody would much mind; but the threat may frighten them for the moment."
>
> "Wasting time is another method of obstruction… the simplest method is Boring. Talk slowly and indistinctly, at a little distance from the point. While you are engaged in Boring it does not matter much what you talk about; but, if possible, you should discourse upon the proper way of doing something which you are notorious for doing badly yourself. Thus… if you are not a good business man, you should discuss the principles of finance and so on… You will make six words do duty for one… and fill up the time until you can think of something to say by talking…"

**On clarity…** Later in this book (Sections 4 and 9) we talk more about the importance of being clear about where we're headed (goals) and "who's gotta do what by when" (roles and responsibilities), and communicating these clearly. When this doesn't happen, conflict is nigh:

> *Most of the strife I've observed (and no doubt contributed to) in organisations I have worked in has arisen from us not being clear about what we need to get done, and who's responsible for what.*

**No popularity contest…** The existence of conflict makes it very clear that being at the head of an organisation or group is not easy. Nor is it a reflection of universal admiration and approval!

With conflict comes unpopularity. The decision-maker may often be criticised more than the actual decision, particularly where there is perceived disadvantage to an individual or a group:

> "A man who dies without enemies is a man who has changed nothing and most probably contributed little in his lifetime." Walter Murdoch (1874–1970)

> *Once you have made decisions and are acting on these, don't worry that people will criticise you or try to undermine you. Don't take this personally or be offended – accept this is as part of the change process.*

Noting that, personally, this can be very uncomfortable…

> *If you're a human being you don't like to be disliked, and especially not hated. I'm a human being too.*

> *The hardest thing I learned is that you can't, ever, keep everyone happy. It was a problem for me, as I like being liked.*

> *It can be very difficult to get people to support you. Be prepared to get all sorts of negative feedback. It will be nasty. It was very difficult for me.*

> *Be careful in looking at what is written about yourself. Whether it's from the internal newsletters, blogs or the local media. You don't need to read all the 'bad news'. Control the inflow of stuff that keeps you awake at night.*

But on the plus side, our experience is that most dark clouds have silver linings:

> *Conflict situations can often provide a good opportunity to turn negative thinking into positive strategies.*

> *The power that I do have is to call people to the table. People with nominally polarised views. I give them a space where*

> *they can talk with some safety. We put aside stuff we can't agree on and focus on the things that we can do something about, and reach a solution.*

Sterling advice.

And remember... of the handful of Golden Rules, one most certainly is: "Where there is conflict in life, there are always two sides to every story."

## 3. The difficulty of COLLABORATION and boundary crossing

> "How easily men could make things better than they are – if only they tried together." Winston Churchill (1874–1965)

> *Most of the smart people around are not in your own organisation.*

**Holding hands in the traffic...** Many lessons about life have been instilled in us from an early age. Robert Fulghum's thought-provoking and pithy best-seller *All I Really Need to Know I Learned in Kindergarten* records that these wisdoms – for nations as well as for individuals and organisations – were found "not at the top of the graduate school mountain, but there in the sandpit at pre-school". Thus we are expected "to play fair... clean up your own mess... say sorry when you hurt somebody" – and lots more.

Fulghum also takes us back to when we were five or six years old, and our teacher led us on an exciting outing, to the fire station or the chocolate factory: "When you go out into the world, watch out for traffic, hold hands, and stick together." Never a truer word. There's a lot of heavy traffic out there.

> *We still, and continually, need to be asking our front line colleagues, at all levels: 'Who are you holding hands with? Who are the best of the best in your line? When did you last interact with them? When are they coming to visit?'*

So it's all about team stuff: 'T.E.A.M. – Together Everyone Achieves More', as the old saying goes. We are, after all…

"…each of us angels with only one wing; and we can only fly by embracing one another." Luciano de Crescenzo (1928– ), Italian writer, film actor, director and engineer.

**Collaboration is not the easy option…** Unfortunately the prevailing culture is, by and large, not supportive of extensive collaboration. There appears to be a form of generic resistance…

*Professional workers can be profoundly bad at collaboration – the performance drivers are usually geared towards individual attainment.*

*One of the things I do most of is trying to persuade people to put aside self-interest to achieve a better outcome.*

*I hear strong and successful collaborators harshly criticised with 'How do we know they are good in their own right if they've done all their work with others?'*

*It's really hard getting people to understand why collaboration is so important and that these are higher-order skills they need to acquire. They can acknowledge this intellectually, but every fibre in their body (and their experience, and history) is pointing diametrically in the other direction.*

It may, of course, be that those who would be affected have no experience (or only limited experience) of collaborating in meaningful ways. As a consequence the leader often has to go out on a limb, and proactively, to push through in this arena.

*We continuously underestimate the tendency and ability of individuals and groups to silo themselves. And we still have to work very hard to get communication across groups that we thought were communicating.*

> *Particularly important in many organisations is the need to operate with what Jack Welch, when CEO at General Electric, called 'boundarylessness' – the need is exceeded only by the difficulty in doing so.*

> *If I had my time again I'd put even more time and effort into breaking down silos.*

**The System – help or hindrance?...** It is also far from clear whether or not the systems in which professionals operate are intrinsically helpful or, in fact, provide some form of inherent obstacles:

> *The world has become so much more complex, with so much more access to information. So much is happening and so many ideas are generated across the 'horizontal', yet we're still dealing with management systems that operate, and get fed, from the vertical.*

> *So much in the system works against collaboration: the organisational setting, the disciplines' own tradition, the financing system, the performance metrics, the professionals themselves – everything. It's a miracle when multidisciplinary initiatives succeed!*

> *By and large, people work together well because of personal chemistry and cohesion of interests rather than because they are directed to do so. However, structure and management can facilitate and enable more such interactions or – more often – can impede them.*

> *Today's successful innovation is 'multi-everything' – culture, institution, nation, product, market. People who are (going to be) successful in our world can operate across systems, languages, governments – we often don't nurture this enough in our organisations. And we certainly don't seem to teach it in our educational establishments. It's mostly still all about extremely 'deep but narrow'.*

But enhancing collaboration is an arena where access to resources can be a very powerful driver. Enhanced resourcing can be used both to support the initiation of collaboration and to promote its maintenance, and even to encourage intellectual jumps that cross previously obstructive boundaries.

*Money is about the only real driver I've got to encourage collaboration. So I say: "If you want strong and tangible institutional support you've got to show us who you are seriously collaborating with."*

**Collaboration can create real benefits...** Collaboration may not be easy; it may be resisted; it may face inherent system-based difficulties, but in the long run it can provide vitality and creativity.

"The most important knowledge is not inside the boundaries of a company. You don't achieve it through containerization, you achieve it through collaboration." Don Tapscott (1947– ) Canadian business executive, author and consultant.

Boundaries emerge when colleagues build 'Chinese walls' around their areas of responsibility and/or expertise, inhibiting both information flow and the possibility of shared understanding. These boundaries are not just those between operational areas within the organisation; increasingly, they also embrace the boundaries between services and other activities outside the organisation. Not only is internal collaboration important in itself but it can also send out strong messages to those outside about the organisation's ability to encourage external collaboration.

All boundaries need to be made transparent and permeable to ideas and influence. This can be a very enriching process, both for individuals and for the organisation:

*Most exciting innovation happens at those strange interfaces between the disciplines. Don't hesitate to send your best people out (sometimes over their strong objections) to visit, and work with, other organisations, working in areas about which they know little. Often they see things that those closer to the operations have missed, and in my organisation's case, this approach led to some important advances.*

*It's amazing the stuff you stumble across working outside your own immediate discipline.*

Notwithstanding the fact that many professional services providers find that more – not less – specialisation is required by their clients, we firmly believe that most value-adding innovation will emerge from activities that lie in the gaps between disciplines:

*Great creativity often emerges from the periphery, whether the periphery is geographical, disciplinary, or cultural.*

**Collabronauts – the 'Cats' of the future?...** So, despite these difficulties, there are strong signs that the future belongs to the boundary crosser and skilled collaborator. Rosabeth Moss Kanter of Harvard University has elegantly coined a spacefaring analogy by introducing the concept of 'collabronauts', who are...

*"...good at making connections, both human and intellectual. They are constantly on the look-out for new ways to benefit from combining forces with partners. They venture into unfamiliar territory, make deals, and return with knowledge that transforms their home base. They bring organisations closer together, introduce people and build relationships among groups that can initially seem like aliens to one another. They manage rumours, mount peace-keeping missions and solve problems. They convince their colleagues to forget old rules and try something new, something that comes with having partners."*

*I agree with Harvard neuroscientist Jason Mitchell who reflected that the most dramatic innovation introduced with the rollout of the human species is not the prowess of individual minds but the ability to harness that prowess across many individuals.*

## UNDERSTANDING THE CULTURE – In Conclusion

The culture of the typical 'cats' environment is often replete with remarkable intellects, and with passion, argument, politics (with a small 'p') and prejudice – mostly based on an inheritance from the different disciplines that have influenced those populating the environment. If these characteristics conflict with your own work-life philosophies, you will probably not be comfortable; indeed you are likely to be frustrated. Accept and embrace these qualities of your cats and you will find the enjoyment of your work life greatly enhanced.

Cultural development is often closely linked with, and nuanced by, particular aspects of an organisation's history. This must be understood – and be seen to be understood – if you are to take a lead in institutional progress. Transformation is far from easy – it can be all-consuming and a long journey. Like marriage, it is not to be taken on 'lightly, wantonly or inadvisedly'.

Bureaucracy can too easily predominate, despite its being abhorrent to many practising professionals. Themselves often bureaucrats at heart, too many can become embroiled in time-consuming trivia. Tread warily, and with careful forethought, but the successful elimination of inappropriate 'red tape' can win both plaudits and improved institutional efficiency.

The future will increasingly be characterised by crossing conventional boundaries (some might say transgressing them) and breaking down desperately-defended silos. But this – and multi-party collaboration, large and small – is DIFFICULT. Persist. Evangelise. And gradually (perhaps even by stealth) reshape your organisational systems and measures of individual and organisational performance to reinforce collaborative behaviour and enhance the culture. Seek out and reward early 'movers and shakers'. The benefits in enhanced vitality, creativity and productivity will thrill.

## B: GETTING THE JOB DONE

Leadership is all about getting results. You stand or fall by your ability to get the job done.

How you do it will be personal.

There are challenges, of course, common to any leadership assignment, whether it be managing a professional partnership, running the fire brigade or being a university dean. We have, therefore, chosen to address a range of issues which include: setting priorities and managing your time; taking decisions and delegating responsibilities; dealing with failure and understanding yourself; managing performance, and handling financial setbacks.

But the 'cats' environment, in our experience and through our observation, can add an overlay of intrigue and complexity. For example, decision making – however sound, necessary and fact-based – can initiate what amounts to trench warfare. You're dealing with intelligent people, many of whom believe they know more than you do about nearly everything. And with so much time spent – and possibly wasted – in ubiquitous committee meetings and discussion groups, effective management towards results can be an art form.

### 4. Taking CHARGE

Leading and managing begin in earnest on the day that you take up your new duties, either through taking up a new post from outside or by being promoted internally. However, you will almost certainly be thinking about your new role from the day when you are appointed – indeed, probably well before that, as you prepared for the interview process.

**First impressions count...** For those moving to a new organisation: you will at the outset gain a great deal of knowledge about that organisation and about those who will be your new colleagues. Here – or, equally, if you are taking up a new role in your current organisation – as a new leader you have a narrow opportunity window to make a good impression. Especially the first time round. Then you're stuck with the old maxim: "You never get a second chance to make a first impression."

The first days need to be approached with care, taking into account not only the particular knowledge you have gained about the new environment and your new responsibilities, but also the range of skills that you have learned over the years in the various posts you will have held as you moved up the professional ladder.

> *There are some things that I knew at the start and have just been unchanging: the need to be enthusiastic but reasonable, the need to have a sound grasp of fundamentals and being able to discuss things meaningfully across a range of topics.*
>
> *Trust your instincts, but be prepared to revisit them in the light of experience.*

In making these first impressions, peer credibility can be important; professionals respect other successful professionals. In contrast…

> *It's hard to lead a charge if you look funny on a horse.*
>
> *You've got to have credibility, and their respect, and show that you are on their side, batting for them. Then they'll move mountains for you. Alignment, trust and respect are key to getting anything done.*

## Out and about…

> *There's a real danger in sitting in your office, and not moving around much. Getting out there builds relationships; and people 'just telling you stuff' is often very valuable.*

A lot has been written about 'managing by walking about'. It applies as much to 'herding cats' as it does in the more general business arena. Thus, the 'leader' who lives primarily in his or her office will usually be seen as remote. This will be reinforced if individuals are 'summoned to the presence'. Of course, when several of the management team are involved, the logical place to get together is in a central office or conference room. On the other hand, 'going walkabout' to see colleagues in their own offices can be really advantageous in a variety of ways: it helps you understand their situation, it encourages approachability and, most usefully, it allows easier control of the length of the exchange. It is also beneficial for your colleagues' staff to see you 'out and about'.

> *In my first week – I remember well all those years back – one of the top bosses called (himself!) – and from 'on high' (the 11th floor) – to say "Hi, and welcome", and fixed a time to come and see me in my shoebox office. I was surprised, and delighted. I joined his fan club that day and would always go out of my way to help him.*

Walking about also enables ready contact with colleagues and staff at all levels, and often provides valuable sources of insight and information...

> *Speak to people openly across the organisation, from the cleaner to the person fixing your computer, to your colleagues... you can learn a lot about what works and what doesn't work throughout the organisation, from people at all levels, by just listening.*

> *In relation to walking the talk... forget it if you think you can run the show, and change things, from your office, by email or through social media. Your people need to see that you're interested – see you talking to people, and watch what you do.*

**Reality will be different...** While advance preparation will obviously stand you in good stead, not least in any job interview process, too much preparation – perhaps leading to some not-necessarily-valid preconceived ideas – may not be helpful:

> *I'm not sure I'd have liked to know too much ahead of time. I learned most, and quickly, from the experiences I've had, from the mistakes I've made, from observing others – very carefully – and from being thrown in the deep end.*
>
> *The second day in the job I realised that I was actually on 'the bridge', and in charge. Despite assiduously preparing for six months, I realised that I knew very little about 'the ship'. The preparation to do something and the reality of actually doing it are different.*
>
> *Appointment bodies tend to emphasise the positives – especially, when they have agreed that 'you're the one', and move into sell mode; the reality will be different. Rarely is there deception – more commonly it's naivety. But you soon find out about the warts you have inherited.*

It is also important to recognise that your learning time cannot be too prolonged – you must quite quickly become engaged with the core business. And the early actions and decisions you take will undoubtedly send important messages:

> *If possible you need an early incident which makes evident the critical point around intent – in my case this was the decision to close a department which was well known to be unacceptably weak.*

**On managing your time (and your priorities)...** In any new role there will be heavy demands imposed upon you. This makes it imperative that you understand how best to manage your time, and this in turn means that you must be able to prioritise your commitments. This is often an area where there is a need to learn fast.

> *Better time management is something I wish I'd learned when I set out on my leadership path.*
>
> *One of the best pieces of advice I ever got, from a very wise and significant leader, was that when you get to start managing/leading bigger stuff, you only need to worry*

*about two things: Look after your health, and look after your time.*

All too often the 'apparently urgent' can crowd out the important. There are many different approaches to prioritisation but, to be effective, there must be a place for both the large and the small issues. One such approach, advocated by the author Stephen Covey, is built upon the notion of packing rocks of varying size into a jar. Put the sand (small issues) in first and the 'big rocks' (the important things) won't fit in or get dealt with. Put the big rocks in first and it is quite surprising how the rest can be accommodated!

*One of the three signs I have on my desk is a card a kind pal sent during one of my frenetic phases: 'A year from today, will it matter?' This proved to be an excellent filter for the 'big rocks' versus the rest.*

## The work-life balance...

*We recruit people who are ambitious, want work that will challenge and stretch them, and are willing to go the extra mile. But we also know that these positive attributes also make them particularly vulnerable to losing balance in their lives.*

*Enjoying work makes for a fulfilled life. Variety and challenge draw many people to a professional career and are what can make it so engaging. But the danger is that work can too readily dominate lives. There is always something more that could be done, or done better, given more time, and competitive pressures drive people in that direction. And in the long run – while this might be seen to help convert ambition into success – many will regret these choices and the negative fall-out can be not just personal but impact careers, colleagues and, ultimately, the organisations for whom they work.*

*Ten years on and I don't have a very good balance between work and the rest of my life... I have had an appendectomy and back surgery, don't exercise, and am about 15 pounds overweight. I have a wife who works long hours and has been too patient about our lack of time together.*

*During and since leaving business school, getting impossible amounts of work done became a perverse source of pride and a way to keep testing myself; and not even having my five-year old daughter chase me down the street begging me not to go to work was able to shift my focus.*

It is very clear that there are increasing pressures on all practising professionals to try to juggle the conflicting demands of activities in the workplace and those of their private and personal lives. These demands impinge on staff at all levels of organisations, from those seeking to establish themselves in their early professional careers to those with a wealth of experience who are taking leading managerial and strategic roles. The work-life balance is an issue which cannot be sidestepped or 'put on the back burner'. It must be addressed and it is not just a 'once in a while' issue.

*I don't much like the distinction/separation implied in the 'work-life balance' debate. Work is part of life, and many of us derive a lot of satisfaction and intellectual pleasure from our work world – and, indeed, from the value-adding relationships in our social life. This makes it an important concern for us to reflect on.*

*Separating work and family life can be false – especially in this age of widespread and constant communication. It's really not clear where one starts and the other ends. And is that necessarily bad? So do recognise that there is the connection.*

"I recall the constant exhaustion of trying to survive on as little as three hours sleep and the sensation of always being one step ahead of disaster. I didn't want to give up sooner in the sense that, in an important job at just 33, I was being looked up to as a role model. I didn't want to be an example to young women that it wasn't possible to have a family and do a high-pressure job. So I worked hard to keep both work and family on the agenda." Gaby Hinsliff (1971– ), former political editor of *The Observer*.

*One of the most worrying trends in some professional services firms is the perceived need to put in 'face time' – where staff feel like they need to be in the office – to be seen even if they don't have work that needs to be done, or if the work can be done from home. As a leader, it is important to show that flexibility can work in professional services and still allow clients to be serviced at the highest levels.*

Overall, the differing demands must be recognised but it is important that a proper balance be maintained – even though that balance may fluctuate from time to time. Professional organisations are now focusing to a significant degree on how people can effectively manage their stress and identify ways in which they can maintain their health and wellbeing while at work. For example, exploring ways in which people can adopt a more flexible approach to their work by experimenting with working from home and other different work patterns.

*We do have some way to go before some of the new approaches to the work-life balance issue are adopted as part of our firm's mainstream culture. But there is a growing acceptance that these issues are not going to disappear.*

**Stakeholder management...** Professional organisations and institutions engage with a wide and demanding number of stakeholders, most notably with clients, but also, for example, with immediate colleagues in sister partnerships, captains (or maybe lieutenants) of industry, and those in the corridors of Government. All must be embraced, so that their separate requirements can be considered and analysed. Needs must be recognised and strategies for fulfilling those needs must be identified.

> *There are two key things to a successful project outcome: the utter confidence of your clients and the loyalty and commitment of those supporting you and working with you.*
>
> *The assessment of value and the competitive nature of a law firm practice brings out the best and the worst. Sadly, we continue to measure value in financial terms. We record units of time based on rates and then charge according to the time recorded and not the actual value. This brings out the worst in people as they strive to record all our time on a matter. We then take this formula (which one has to surmise was developed by either a lawyer or an accountant) and place it in an environment that is doubly competitive. Internally amongst lawyers, and externally against other service providers. The real measure must be based on whether clients like the service supplied and the value ascribed to it and come back for more. The ultimate compliment in the service sector must surely be repeat business!*

In achieving the best relationships with clients, there is no doubt that a 'one size fits all' response won't work. Solutions must match needs, and this requires gaining a very clear understanding of the many and varying characteristics of the needs involved. Often, achieving this understanding will make it necessary for you to consider issues from the point of view of the stakeholder, just as much as from the point of view of your own organisation.

> *Don't underestimate – or neglect – your stakeholders; we are sometimes inclined to assume we know more than they do.*
>
> *Don't go and tell your key stakeholders what you want to do, and what you want from them. Listen to what they're interested in, and then make the connections with your objectives. Then you'll have their interest, and support.*

Very often Government is a major stakeholder. But you don't do business with Government – only with people. All contact should be an exercise in, and an opportunity for, relationship-building and for establishing mutual respect, mutual value-add, and mutual trust. If, additionally, you and your counterpart get to like each other, that can be a real bonus. And, as in most relationships, communication is a key issue in both form and content. This can often demand acts of self-denial...

> *A very senior politician once said to me, no doubt off the record: "Those darn professionals are all the same – just like little birds in a nest, always chirping, with their mouths open, and asking for more!"*

But just because your Government stakeholders often have financial clout does not mean that your other, non-government stakeholders are less important. Quite the contrary – balancing competing demands is a skill that needs to be acquired.

Re-emphasising the point: it is critical to build strong relationships with your clients...

> *Years on, when I was asked to summarise the key to the most-would-say-successful organisational survival and transformation process I had had the privilege of leading, I said it could be distilled into one word: "Relationships, relationships, relationships". (Okay, I never was much good at arithmetic.)*

### People and your time...

> "Time spent with cats is never wasted." Sigmund Freud (1856–1939)

> *Getting results is about understanding the people around you as much as you can, and helping them get the best out of their efforts.*

> *As a preamble re approaching the job, I try to divide the issues which partners come to you with into three: Nasty; has to be dealt with immediately. Insoluble; been around a long time, people brighter than you have tried to resolve it (so don't worry if you can't – it's okay to have some insolubles*

> *which people gnaw on, as long as they're not corrosive). Then lastly, those where you listen, and say "That's a really good point – go and speak to X, Y, Z and have you thought of A, B, C? And let's speak again next week." They never come back next week.*

Management/leadership is a full-on people business and our Section 8 focuses on this area. Initially you will need to engage both with your immediate colleagues and with staff at many different levels in your organisation.

> *I spend a lot of time with my people, especially if they are new and recruited from the outside, talking about the culture of our organisation: how we do things around here, how we operate and how we make decisions.*

> *When I started running an organisation, although I realised that people issues were important, I still did not realise how much time they would take up.*

> *I wish that someone had sat me down and asked me if I was ready to expend most of my energy on the development and growth of others in the service of the shared vision. I wish that I had been told this rather than discovering it by accident.*

And, as mentioned above, there will also be contacts and stakeholders requiring your personal time, and this may mean that you need to draw upon quite different approaches from those used inside the organisation. Here you cannot assume the levels of knowledge of 'the system' that many of your colleagues have. This all takes time and there are no easy shortcuts. However, there are aids to progress – and pitfalls to be avoided.

Thus, whether you are interacting 'outside' or 'inside' your organisation, some common wisdoms apply. For example…

> *Try to learn people's names.*

# B: GETTING THE JOB DONE

*Building credibility and respect takes ten times longer than losing it.*

*People infer as much from what you don't say as they do from what you actually do say.*

*You don't have to show off and try to prove how clever you are: "I don't understand; this is beyond my capabilities" is better. As is making fun of yourself.*

And don't be afraid to ask 'stupid' questions since there are no such things. The Scots have a wonderful, 'third-party' approach which is to ask the 'daft laddie' question. Instead of using a self-deprecating approach: "… this may be a stupid question, but why are you doing A and not B…?", they frequently adopt the line: "…a daft laddie might ask why you're doing A rather than B…".

**Getting delegation right…** One very effective way of making your time go further, motivating your team and getting results, is to commit to considered and measured delegation:

*Give people responsibility and don't micromanage; trust them, and value their way of doing things – which inevitably will be different from yours. The outcomes are what count.*

*Don't try to micromanage when they are the experts. You'll lose respect and credibility.*

*Delegating responsibility and then constantly interfering tends to bring out the worst in people.*

*I've learned to be much less of an interferer.*

*Don't delegate and then send emails of advice.*

However, notwithstanding the importance of boundary crossing (and collaboration), those to whom authority is delegated need clarity about where they can – and should – act, and where they shouldn't…

*If you have a square surrounded by busy roads and a group of children playing there, they will migrate to the middle of*

> *the square. If you fence it off (i.e. set clear boundaries) they will use the whole area. Very few organisations do this well, but if you delegate clearly – and about twice as much as you think wise – accepting the occasional breaches and allowing great freedom of decision making within the boundaries, you are most likely to enhance motivation and get strong performance.*

In other words, make sure your colleagues know exactly what they're on the line for, and that what they're doing is important, and that successful outcomes really matter to you. Relatedly, and as part of the framing of your delegation, it is also important to make it clear that you will all have to face consequences if there is undue delay or inaction.

> *To bring out the best in people, it is important to have an agreed common purpose and then provide the maximum amount of autonomy and flexibility to allow partners and staff to operate within those boundaries. If you try to exercise too much control, or don't have a common purpose or business reason behind your decisions, you will spend a lot of time debating decisions and demotivating people. You might spend time debating decisions anyway, but at least people will be more likely to have a common language and understand that your decisions are coming from a business perspective.*

Further, there will be times when the need for formal delegation comes unexpectedly:

> *Good people will attract external commitments, often at short notice ("You need to join the Chairman in Singapore on Tuesday."). This can often make the management of day-to-day life quite complex.*

All the more reason, therefore, to ensure that good delegation processes are in place, and that your team/direct reports are quality and 'in the loop'. (See also Sections 8 and 9.)

**Managing duality...** In this complex, pressured, ambiguous and dilemma-filled world, we need to work with the 'and', not the 'or'. Thus, for example, it is usually best to nurture diverse perspectives, but these need to be channelled. We must be competitive but work in partnerships, action-oriented but reflective, planned but opportunistic. Change is critical, but so is the stability provided by continuity. Analysis is key, but so is making use of your intuition. Organisationally, we can appropriately centralise but also empower through decentralisation; be 'big' in scope and power but 'small' in terms of responsiveness.

*The leader needs to be comfortable wearing 'bifocal glasses'... being comfortable looking into the future AND, at the same time, being able to ensure that today's results are delivered. Because without a successful today there may be no truly effective tomorrow for the organisation.*

*The leader needs to harness schizophrenia... in the ballroom analogy – on the floor dancing but also up on the balcony observing.*

**Quality decision making...** It is necessary to accept at a very early stage that, for all the areas where you are 'on the line', ultimately, you are principally responsible for the decisions that determine courses of action. There may be, and usually is, a collectivity of inputs. There may be delegation. But, at the end of the day, while the ownership can be shared, the 'buck' stops on the leader's desk. So...

*Learn to focus on the 'so whats' of a project (the outcomes if successful)... not just the 'whats'. This is the essence of being a successful professional leader/manager rather than just an apparatchik.*

*Never agree to a proposal without thinking through the consequences.*

*What brings out the worst in our people is arbitrary, non-evidenced-based and/or inconsistency in decision making.*

Even so...

*What distinguishes a great leader from a good leader is their intuition.*

*Timing is all; and chance matters.*

It is appropriate to trust gut feelings. Dr Ramesh Mashelkar, an elder statesman of Indian science, tells a very relevant story around a patent challenge in which he makes quite clear how an important decision was (actually) made:

> "How was this decision to challenge the patent taken? I remember reading the *Times of India* in my home in Delhi as I was having a cup of tea in the morning. I saw this news item. Some innovators from a university in the USA had been granted a patent on the wound-healing properties of turmeric. I was shocked. This was something that had been known in India for generations. Since it was prior knowledge, it did not fulfil the criteria of novelty, non-obviousness and utility, which are a must for the granting of a patent. I intuitively decided to fight it. I made a public announcement that same evening as a part of a public lecture at the National Physical Laboratory in Delhi. This was daring. I was Secretary to the Government of India, therefore I should have ideally secured several government permissions before announcing the challenge publicly. But I went entirely by my intuition and instincts and just announced the challenge. The rest is history – the patent was disallowed."

Additionally, honesty and transparency in decision making (and related communication) are also key. It tends to go down badly when there is (perceived) dishonesty or flummery around decisions, for example when questions are rightly asked around who actually took the decision, and why.

*Clever people are much more willing to accept decisions they don't like if they are given a reasonable reason for the*

> *decision. Sometimes – even quite often – this will mean giving the objector some background information that he or she didn't have – often through circumstance, not through fault. So you need to have your antennae quite well-tuned to where the 'objecting audience' is coming from.*
>
> *People want an answer – even if they don't like it. Avoiding taking the call, or ambiguity, is weak leadership. What people hate most is uncertainty.*

Inactivity can frustrate. Don't take lack of complaint as support for inaction – often people merely sigh, and get on with their own thing. For this reason…

> *I've found that a willingness to make decisions is welcomed even if the decisions aren't to everyone's liking.*
>
> *I remember, when I was newly appointed, the leaders who commanded greatest respect among my (then) colleagues were the ones who showed flexibility – a sense of not being hidebound by rules, but willing to make bold decisions on the basis of commonsense (and facts!), and to accept responsibility for the outcome. They were also decisive. We knew where we stood. They would listen carefully to a proposal and then make a decision (often involving disbursement from discretionary funds).*

Issues must be grasped and not evaded:

> *Some leaders I've observed can be reluctant to take the really hard decisions: "Why do today what you can put off until tomorrow?" In consequence, the problems accumulate, or grow, over time because nobody is taking the tough calls.*

Even people with apparent long-term appointments can live by this maxim, by the way! But, (re)emphasising the point, beware the inappropriate delay – which may have a variety of origins…

> *Some leaders promoted from functional specialisation – and therefore out of their comfort zone – are sometimes reluctant*

> to lead and to make a decision if they don't have complete consensus. Professionals can be very skilled at 'constructive delays'.
>
> Leaders tend to underestimate the time and cost of decisions which are untimely, or where they don't actually make the decision at all. I see it all the time in my work – many of my clients in the public sector are paralysed with fear about making decisions. This is partly a legacy culture issue, e.g. decision making by committee, and partly due to the ever-increasing personal risk for public sector leaders in the current political and economic environment.

Deciding whether or not to consult can also be problematic.

> You need to be very clear, and distinguish carefully between when you should (just) inform, versus consult, versus negotiate. They are quite different. And you should clearly signal which line you intend to follow, so that everybody knows.
>
> Sometimes you need to take the line: "The buck stops with me, and I've heard what you've all said, and now I'm making the decision." If this is said and done in a good way it can even be cheerfully accepted by the team.
>
> Engagement and consultation are important – but there comes a time where you need to decide and get on with implementation. Realising that can be very liberating.
>
> Your people need to see that – whatever you decide – you've listened seriously to all (relevant) points of view. You have to consult, but you have to decide.

And after the decision is taken it will usually be necessary to stand firm.

> I was very influenced by a wonderful leader I once had who was a great change agent... and would make decisions, never if there was only narrow support but often if support was maybe a 70:30. Only once did all the '30 percents' coalesce

> *into some quite fierce opposition. She was unmoved, stating that the only thing that the opposition had in common was dislike of her!*

There will, of course, be occasions when it quite quickly becomes apparent that a decision that has been taken is wrong in part or in whole. Then it is best to acknowledge that and revisit the original decision. The worst course is to 'die in the ditch' and stubbornly persist with the erroneous position. Seeking to save face can be a real mistake.

**Handling failure...** Although it would be admirable if every aspect of your role ran smoothly and successfully, this is usually – indeed very much – the exception rather than the rule...

> *In every highly professional organisation you get mistakes, and things fail. You need to be emotionally and intellectually prepared for this.*

But...

> *Blaming others for failures... is a certain path to perdition.*
>
> *Hanging someone out to dry when there has been a mess-up is a mistake. Clearly if and when there are persistent errors you need to deal with poor performance. But taking responsibility as the leader, and defending your team from unwarranted attack will send an important message of your support to the rest of your troops.*
>
> *True leadership is most clearly revealed when others on your team make mistakes.*
>
> *As a leader you need to take responsibility for failure. And celebrate everyone else when there's success.*
>
> *When somebody fails, getting into the blame game is a disaster. Assuming it's not negligence, it's about saying "What have we learned from this? – How can I help you, going forward?"*

It is this latter sentiment that must be overriding.

> "He who has never failed somewhere, that man cannot be great." Herman Melville (1819–1891)

**Goal and role clarity...** In addition – and closely related – to the ubiquitous 'communication problems' (see Section 9), conflict in the workplace can arise for a variety of reasons. Two, in particular. First, non-clarity around goals: "You think we should be headed there, but I think it should be over here...". Second, non-clarity around roles: "You think this is my job; I think it's yours..." Thus, clarifying just exactly where we're headed and 'Who's going to do what by when' can save a lot of time and trouble.

In practice, therefore, it is apparent that...

> *Having high and clearly-articulated objectives... brings out the best in people.*

**Knowing yourself...** So far we have concentrated primarily on the interactions between the leader/manager and his or her team, and the circumstances in which he or she is operating. While the need for self-knowledge has been implicit in those discussions, it is important to make some more explicit observations:

> *When you know yourself well there are some things or behaviours you might need to suppress... If you are inclined to be pessimistic, suppress it – people need their leader to be optimistic about the future. (As a wise leader once said, to me: "My job is to absorb uncertainty, and stop my people from being scared".) If you have a tendency to panic, suppress it – what you do and how you behave as a leader will be magnified, and they will think 'things must really be bad'. If you're somewhat introverted, suppress it – get out there and 'work the room' as it's part and parcel of your leadership responsibilities.*

But it's not all simply black and white. Taking note of the greyness can be valuable...

The doubts you have are useful – to inform your current situation, and to be realistic about future possibilities.

> *Many leaders suffer from the impostor syndrome..."Can I really do this? It's surely just a matter of time before someone finds me out?" Knowing it wasn't just me – earlier – would have been reassuring.*
>
> *Ask yourself regularly: "Am I still committed to my goals?"*

And if you are looking to lead...

> *Leadership has to be intentional if it is to be effective – although one might inadvertently, or accidentally, or even belligerently end up in a leadership role. To lead without intent is a dangerous place.*
>
> *You need to be very clear, in your own mind, why you want the leadership position. And what it is you're looking for. I wanted to make change happen.*
>
> *What motivated me to get into a leadership role in the first place? To do it better than I'd seen it done.*
>
> *There's a difference between leadership and authority. In our business even juniors are encouraged to accept responsibility, and take leadership. Authority you only get through the recognition of those around you – based on your demonstrated experience, and perhaps even acquired wisdom. You gain the authority that they grant you.*
>
> *Time in a leadership position only reinforces what one knew at the start – but it's so important – integrity is everything. You lead by permission, not by rank or authority. You lose that permission if your motives are doubted.*
>
> *Leadership translates into high visibility in all things that you do. If you do not want visibility do not lead. Knowing this is an important part of the decision-making process*

> *that we often do not have the opportunity to consider before becoming a leader.*

**The value of networking...** The more senior you get, the lonelier it (often) becomes.

> *It would have been good to have been warned about the loneliness of leadership before I experienced it.*

Having an external network, which includes people who have 'been there, done that' and can act as informal mentors, can be very valuable. Participation with colleagues and peers from different organisations, or different parts of your own organisation – for example, in leadership development training – can build a long-lasting support and advice network. Working with kindred spirits who have empathetic shoulders to cry on when it's crying time can be beneficial.

Networking also better enables us to benchmark, for example:

- Are we suffering from hubris?
- Are we as good as we think – and say – we are?
- Are we as well-connected as we should be?

> *Since taking up the top job here, I've visited a number of my opposite numbers running similar organisations – and it's one of the best time-investments I've made. For example, cross-calibrating around what's 'hot' in our type of business, and comparing notes on the trials and tribulations of herding cats. And looking for opportunities to work together – I'm pushing all my executive to do the same. I'm preaching 'network, network, network'.*

'Outside' visits – even (and sometimes especially!) in one's own organisation – can be exceedingly valuable. Three things can happen:

- Hitherto unidentified opportunities for collaboration may emerge.

- Objective feedback or advice on problems can help hugely (and comes for free).
- 'Creative plagiarism': "That's a very good idea, I'll try it in my place."

Push hard, therefore, at encouraging networking, but with the full understanding that...

> *As you encourage your good people to network and work collaboratively, their own talent will get spotted and temptations (to leave) will surely come their way. C'est la vie. You then just have to work harder to help them excel and be happy with you.*

**Building trust...** Trust is important; very important. You build trust in small, bite-sized chunks, but you can destroy it in one fell swoop. As we say elsewhere: trust is the air that good relationships breathe.

> *I'm very cautious in my people- and culture-related decisions. It takes a day to mess up morale, and a year to fix it. Inclusivity and transparency are key – harder work but a better chance of success.*

> *You demonstrate trust by delegating responsibility appropriately (and here, think 'more not less') and through showing loyalty in standing by your staff member when they don't deliver the outcome you'd hoped for, despite their best efforts.*

> *If the project succeeds, the project leader is on the podium. If it fails I'm on the podium. People have got to know: we are behind you and we believe in you.*

**On power...** There is often a temptation to believe that, as a leader, you are in charge and your position is one of power and influence. This is, of course, true to some extent, but...

> *The idea that you are there in absolute control is totally misleading.*

*Leading in our environment is an odd role. Most of the pleasures – and they are real – are vicarious, experienced through the successes of others; most of the achievements are by stealth.*

"The presidential power that seems so vast and indeed so excessive to many outside the White House appears all too small and shrunken to presidents and their aides when compared to the stupendous burdens put on the White House." James MacGregor Burns (1918– )

**And a final thought…** Whatever you do, don't pretend to know when you don't – you will always be found out. And your credibility will be lost.

*Saying "I don't know" or "Please explain this to me", in other words admitting your ignorance, can be a good thing – far from being seen as failure, people like explaining things to the boss.*

## 5. COMPOSURE under pressure and the implementation imperative

"Genius is one percent inspiration, and ninety-nine percent perspiration." Thomas Edison (1847–1931)

**Sticking to the game plan (and staying calm)…** Tenacity and staying power are all-important. Leaders and managers need to have a very strong sense of purpose, combined with an ability to recognise problems as they arise. And when it comes to problems, obey the sign spotted in a local lift: "If there is a problem, stay calm". And remember the old Rudyard Kipling poem which starts "If you can keep your head when all about you are losing theirs, and blaming it on you" – because, as one of our colleagues remarked, "Calmness is a vital, core response skill in a leader".

B: GETTING THE JOB DONE

*To succeed in management around here you need an ordered mind. You can't be a stressful person. You need to be a pretty calm type, to cope with the volume and the short deadlines.*

Also, from the point of view of the team, it is necessary for them to see that you are not easily deflected from the agreed path.

*Because the lead times for successful change to embed are so long, the hardest – and most important – thing, I've found, is sticking to the unrelenting, unwavering belief in our strategy, and riding over the bumps of inevitable perturbation, when sometimes, in the short term, it may look as if you've got it wrong.*

"Leadership is all about composure under pressure and sticking to the game plan." John Eales (1970– ), former Australia rugby captain.

Obviously we're not talking dogmatic 'Charge of the Light Brigade' commitment.

*The change process is like men ballroom dancing – if you never take any steps backwards it's boring.*

Thus you are likely to need to exercise some well-judged flexibility from time to time – one door might shut and another open; there are usually a number of different ways to achieve your overarching goals.

**Plan well...** "Be Prepared" – the Boy Scouts' motto. On the other hand...

"We don't have a plan, so nothing can go wrong." Spike Milligan (1918–2002), British comedian

You need, first, to arm yourself with a sense of purpose, and then, usually, to ensure that there is focused commitment by all the team towards delivery. This needs a delivery plan. An understanding of only the rudiments of project management certainly doesn't mean that you need to hand over the planning responsibility to an 'expert'. However, the exception here would be in mission-critical developments – for example, the literature abounds with reports of major IT projects which have lost their way, gone frighteningly over budget and in the end failed to deliver the planned outcomes because of inexpert management.

> *In putting in a major, new, enterprise-wide information system, I was advised to think 'times pi' – that is: "If you're not careful, it will take you about three times as long as you thought it would, and probably cost three times as much as you budgeted." Anticipating this, we put much better controls around delivery and deadlines, and around budgeting and expenditure.*

It is always worth remembering...

> "Chance favours the prepared mind." Louis Pasteur (1822–1895)

Finding the balance between thoughtfully structured planning within the team and professionally facilitated project management is an art that needs to be worked on.

> *The techniques for managing projects well, whether they are large and transformational or small and incremental, have not varied since Rome was built, but are continually forgotten. In addition to well-structured pre-planning, the most common element forgotten is clear accountability – in other words, clearly assigned follow-up actions and responsibilities.*

> *We should have been more reflective and better planned around the management of our change processes – a key task of leadership.*

But try not to overdo it; sometimes very simple approaches will suffice...

> *The more formal and comprehensive project management methodologies are not usually applicable to our sort of*

*(smaller scale) more specialist environment – we're not building jumbo jets or nuclear reactors. It's not a widely-accepted view, but the backs of envelopes, or napkins in the tea-room, have worked really well in my career. The exception, by observation, being major IT or building projects – then you bring in the serious, professional project managers or you end up in big trouble.*

**Implementation excellence...** Effective execution is an imperative. Ninety-five per cent of all the decisions we take stand or fall on the success – or otherwise – of the quality of the implementation process.

"Vision without execution is hallucination." Thomas Edison (1847–1931)

"A vision is worth little if the President doesn't have the character – the courage and heart – to see it through." Peggy Noonan (1950– ), speech writer for President Ronald Reagan.

*Having a well-articulated view of your operating environment – your 'current reality', as they say – you need to separate out strategic intent (what to do) from strategic execution (how to do it). The latter is almost always more difficult, and where most of us fail.*

*Execution excellence must be an all-out attack... All you need is clarity, ownership, focus and connectedness around just a few key goals, with effective cascading and line of sight 'down' to the individual contributor, with success measures in place and 'cradle to grave' performance management; in other words goals plus measures plus performance review integrated across organisation-unit-individual levels. But, wow, if only it were this easy...!*

*Describe what you're going to do and then live up to it.*

*No matter how elegant the strategic or policy solution (to a problem or opportunity) is, it is worthless unless it can be delivered effectively – separating strategy or policy development from implementation often leads to a poor outcome… You need to have structures and processes in place to systematically connect creative policy development and its execution.*

**Small steps?…** 'How to get there' – the detail of implementation – is often not clear at the start. But the leisure of having time to plan for the great launch is not normally available; it is essential that things start to happen:

*When you don't know how to take the big steps, first take the most sensible little step.*

*Keep the problem grand while making the steps to the solution small… Having colleagues plodding towards a far-off goal will initially be motivating by its scope, but people become disenchanted by its distance unless small goals are met along the way.*

*In the change process, if you have no signs of success within the first year or so then you have failed. You need small success stories all the way along.*

**Organising arrangements…** The conventional wisdom is that 'structure follows strategy'; that is, your operational design should support effective strategy implementation. While modifying your structure may well help you deliver on your strategic goals – potentially more rapidly and effectively than through the prevailing organising arrangements – be careful to look before you leap into extensive restructuring.

By the time they reach senior positions, most leaders will have seen the quotation, often attributed (some would say erroneously) to Petronius Arbiter (27–66 AD):

"We trained hard… but it seemed that every time we were beginning to form up into teams, we would be reorganised. I was to learn later in life that we tend to meet any new situation by reorganising; and a wonderful method it can be for creating the illusion of progress while producing confusion, inefficiency, and demoralisation."

Whether the attribution is correct or not is by the by; the sentiment provides an important cautionary message which it is wise to keep firmly in mind. And remember...

*The more complicated an organisation is, the better communication has to be.*

**Where the devil resides...** While it is tempting as 'the leader' to concentrate only around the 'big picture', this can be risky. An awareness of the ways in which implementation can go wrong is needed, and in most cases this originates among the 'small' things:

*Effective leadership and management of an organisation requires a capacity for attention to detail, and for completing processes so that they will work, for ensuring that functions work, even in the smallest units where services are delivered.*

"Never neglect details." General Colin Powell (1937– )

**And what gets measured...** gets done, so says the old, and useful, adage. But be careful about getting carried away by this sentiment.

"Not everything that can be counted counts, and not everything that counts can be counted." Albert Einstein (1879–1955)

*It is foolish indeed to insist on objectives and targets and measures that then totally prescribe people's behaviour. This is not the way to run a professional service organisation, although it might be the way to run a supermarket – though even then I doubt it.*

'Less is more' – absolutely – when it come to metrics. And it is also essential to ensure, when you use them, that they're meaningful, clearly articulated and well-communicated.

Certainly rather loose metrics are often encountered, but they serve to illustrate the point that there is a need to find useful measurable outcomes. Increasingly, there is a tendency to see the use of 'metrics' as a sort of catch-all solution to measuring implementation effectiveness – even to the point of their becoming an end in themselves. As well as this, irrelevant or inappropriate metrics can be more dangerous than no metrics at all since they can distort the outcomes to meet the requirements of the metrics:

> *Metrics are really difficult. Often huge reliance is placed on them; but professionals don't want to be measured by input and output – they believe they're doing something more special than that. Metrics have their place, but they should never be the sole criteria for judgment.*

> *Metrics need to be relevant and aligned with the values and behaviours you expect from an organisation.*

And let us not forget another old saying: "You tell me how you're going to measure me, and I'll tell you how I'm going to behave."

**Following through on performance is critical...** At the nominal conclusion of the implementation process, it is not sufficient to smile comfortably and simply close the book. There needs to be active follow-up.

> *When I failed, it was when I didn't hold people to account. Maybe giving feedback was too hard, or I didn't make it important enough to invest the time, or they were valuable and I thought I might offend and then lose them. Whatever... It was always a mistake.*

> *I've seen some frustrated guys, late 40s or early 50s, who haven't made it to the top, and won't, even though they'd*

*like to, and probably have the inherent competence to do so. But they were let down by some boss or other, ten or even twenty years before, who failed to be frank and honest with them around some of their key flaws. Fixable back then, but entrenched now. And I've seen other highflyers get frank, no-holds-barred feedback, early in their careers and it strengthens their wings. It worked for me.*

*Striving to be the best we can be requires us to continually seek constructive critiquing and feedback on how we can improve.*

*When someone has already made up their mind that they've got the right answer, it's too late for criticism. It will often then be seen as destructive. You need a process to expose people to critique when the ideas are still developing – and you can add value, or even re-direct. Then the feedback/ criticism is usually seen as constructive. It's a great way to see ideas expand, and people grow. It's a bit like working with building blocks, as opposed to chipping away at something that's already been built.*

Although this is far from easy, it is important, because…

*Professionals and technical specialists tend to be optimistic, therefore they can mislead each other, and themselves. They can have rose-coloured glasses around how good they are.*

**Have patience: it all takes time…** Particularly when you take on organisational change, 'it' always takes much, much longer than you think it will. Remember – as one observer put it – the internet took twenty years to become an overnight success!

*I've now come to realise that what we set out to do could not have been achieved in the tenure of a single Chief Executive.*

*Your achievements probably will not really be known for five to ten years – and they will depend upon how successful your successor is.*

## 6. COMMITTEES and meetings

Committees and working groups are, or can appear to be, the life-blood of many professional communities although practice in the professional world is very varied. Nevertheless, the widespread presence of committees such as Audit, Remuneration, Partnership Matters etc. does mean that they create an arena which needs to be thought about. They are resolutely part of the landscape, but they are not necessarily benign and can proliferate like weeds, and resist abolition.

*I'm an abolisher of committees. Like one of my folk heroes – a politician, as it happens – did when he came into power, I abolished all the committees and made them talk themselves back into existence. Very few of them managed to.*

There is, of course, a place for committees but they must have real work to do, a tight brief, and clear reporting deadlines. You will need to do your homework around the selection of the membership and, particularly, the selection of the Chair. In the professional world, major committees can in fact be…

*…great places for preventing fires starting, by opening up contentious issues. The occasional and well-judged vote can also give you a real sense of the mood, and how strong it is.*

*Some committees are needed in order to provide decision-making mechanisms – but those involved must be well informed – perceptions and attitudes are important – so somewhere along the line it is essential to get the right people involved and consulted – committees can do this.*

But all too often committees don't deliver on expectations:

"The appointment of a [committee] 'to consider what means, if any, can be discovered to prevent the Public Washing of Linen'… [results in] the formation of an invertebrate body which sits for two years, with growing discomfort, on the clothes-basket containing the linen. When the [committee] is so stupefied that it has quite forgotten what it is sitting on, it issues three minority reports, of enormous bulk, on some different subject. The reports are referred to the Council... and [thereafter] to the wastepaper basket. This is called 'reforming the University from within'." Francis Cornford (1874–1943)

Committees are an aid to management and not a substitute for it.

*You can't manage through committees... you can only manage through people.*

*We established a committee to manage cross-institution infrastructure. It didn't work. You need a person in charge.*

And as for managing committee meetings themselves, it is quite surprising how badly this is often done:

"Meetings... made the Mad Hatter's Tea Party seem like a paradigm of positive decision-making." David Lodge (Changing Places, 1975)

**Meetings Management 101...** The most basic advice on running meetings makes it evident that this too is an art form, especially in its chairing. Committee meetings are somewhat different from general 'meetings' per se, but both are part and parcel of getting the job done, whether they are regular meetings of staff and the like, or opportunity- or challenge-focused brain-storming sessions.

And certain 'principles' apply all round:

*First and foremost, around meetings, my mantra is "Do we need a meeting?"*

If the answer is Yes, then you need to clarify the nature of the meeting, and possibly of each particular agenda item. Specifically:

*The purpose of meetings (and agenda items therein) often get confused. For example: Is this a decision-making meeting? Or merely consultation? Or is the meeting (or the agenda*

> *item) just information sharing? Then again, maybe it's just brainstorming.*
>
> *Often, it's very useful to clarify up front: 'What are we talking about here?'.*

Next, if you do need a meeting, who do you need at the meeting? And why?

> *Too often people who don't need to be there are at meetings, wasting your time and theirs. Conversely, when the key decision maker(s) can't make it, everyone else is just marking time.*

Discipline is, therefore, important to a productive meetings culture. Be clear 'from the top' that if Fred can't make a particular session, for whatever reason, he has to live with the decisions and actions resulting from the meeting. And you will need to work hard not to be continuously changing meeting times to accommodate player X, Y or Z:

> *Changing meeting times is a cottage industry around here. It keeps the PAs gainfully employed for maybe half their time!*

Committees do need to meet, so invest quality time beforehand in crafting the agenda. Start, and end, the meeting on time. Nurture inclusivity – encouraging all participants to contribute. To this end, whether you are Chair or just a member, read any necessary papers beforehand.

As with most endeavours, preparation is key. For example, does everyone concerned know what the meeting is about? Has the agenda been circulated in advance? Have any necessary papers also been circulated in advance, giving people enough time to read them... Be righteously indignant if there is an inadequate notice period for advanced digestion. And expect others to be righteously indignant if you slip up in this regard. Progress can be made if careful thought is given to the preparation of the papers for the meeting, especially for those 'big ones'.

# B: GETTING THE JOB DONE

Being really organised can pay dividends:

*We started making some good progress when we restructured and colour-coded the Board papers. We used a cover page (white) – which explained the purpose of the paper and indicated recommendations, with implications. Backup pages (blue) are desirable reading with basic information on background, issue(s) defined, process, conclusions, recommendations, implications – including resourcing requirements, follow-up actions, together with accountabilities and timescales. Supporting pages (pink) provide all the detailed information and data that could be drawn upon to support the Backup pages. We found very quickly that the members of our Board could then better prioritise their approach to meetings.*

One of the important advance tasks for the Chair is to decide who comes to the meeting, fully recognising that they come with different perspectives, have different styles, can contribute in different ways. And these different qualities need to be harnessed.

The Chair plays a key role in stopping people dominating the conversation and in pulling in the often more quiet people to make a contribution…

*One of the problems with meetings is that people often don't listen. They just wait for an opportunity to make their point. One fun thing to do, now and again, is making a rule that you can only talk when you have summarised adequately the point made by the previous person (and to his or her satisfaction). This slows things down of course but has useful consequences.*

The Chair should aim to summarise proceedings after each agenda item, recapping the decisions taken and making explicit the follow-up action required, with clearly-defined roles and responsibilities, and timescales.

The minutes of the meeting should be out in draft form as soon as possible (this really matters) and be given to the Chair to review and turn around in a day. After ratification by the Chair, they should go immediately to the other committee members. Minutes that arrive two days before the next meeting (quite likely a month or so later) are no use: no one will remember whether they are accurate or not, and they cannot act as an action-memo for recalcitrant members who did not make a note of the jobs they were supposed to do.

All this should go without saying – but rarely does.

**Are formal committees a necessary evil?...** Regrettably this would seem to be the case. But, in thinking about committees, you should decide whether they are needed at all. Often a job that needs to be done is time-limited, and in that case the work can be done effectively by an ad hoc working party or task group that is itself time-limited. This can be a step towards simplification and, in this context, there is advantage in keeping the committee arrangements under review.

Despite the downsides, however, one of the beneficial roles a committee can play is that of oversight, fostering a sense of participation, democracy, openness and transparency in decision-making. Ideally, the committee is broadly representative, but may meet only rarely – the work and decision-making in practice being done in summary fashion by the chair of the committee, perhaps with a small ad hoc group, subject to the tacit consent of the whole committee. All such decisions are rapidly (note: rapidly) communicated to the members by email circular. Any member who wishes may object, and request a meeting to consider any of the 'decisions'. If the chair is performing competently and has the respect and confidence of the committee, such objections may be rare, but the real possibility of challenging any decision that is dubious or seems to require further consideration gives a sense of common purpose and joint decision-making.

**Key success factors for review committees...** Quite a different domain is occupied by committees or task forces that are set up to carry out a very specific role – such as a review of the effectiveness of a particular activity. In addition to the careful selection of the participating members, the Key Success Factors for review committees – which might also apply to more general committee work – should include the following:

- A tight brief, agreed beforehand by both the reviewers and those whose activity is being reviewed
- Careful selection of the Chair
- Well-thought-through briefing material. Be prepared to stamp down on any 'overkill' submission from those being reviewed in which absolutely everything is dropped on the unsuspecting reviewers... Remember Mark Twain's ironic observation: "I haven't got time to write you a short letter so I've written you a long letter."
- Rapid turn-around time on the draft report, for member scrutiny and, thereafter, timely finalisation
- Subsequent, senior-level monitoring, for example after six or twelve months, to ensure that the approved recommendations have been, or are being, effectively implemented, and not forgetting to feed this progress back to the review members. Nothing is more galling for a review group than feeling that their hard work and precious time has gone into the proverbial black hole.

**Review fatigue...** If you are not careful, reviewing can become a business in its own right and something of a substitute for management.

*We were, probably indisputably, the best specialist group in our area of expertise in the country. But across seven years we had to run six major reviews. It was just insane.*

**Keep the Chair informed...** Focused reviews can have unpredictable outcomes. At times observations and recommendations are not at all what was expected, and seriously bad news can be uncovered. Whatever the story, never – ever – hide (or 'spin') bad news from members of your governing Board or its equivalent, and especially not from its Chair. If there is trouble around the corner the Chair should be given the courtesy of 'no surprises'. The bad news will always come out, often with an emphasis that makes it seem worse that it really is. Most individuals who rise to this level of governance are pretty aware, and know only too well that, in all organisations, things go wrong. And sometimes very wrong. Trust is the air that good relationships breathe. Not 'telling it how it is' is one sure-fire way to undermine this.

> *You also need to be very clear about getting bad news early – and that hiding things is not acceptable. (They often get worse, anyway!) It's about saying "OK, so now we're going to develop a solution together".*

**On governance and ethics...** This is currently a hot topic especially following the global financial crisis and the 'failure of governance' that seems to make media headlines all too regularly. For example, if you search the internet for 'Harvard Business School and its professors' priority interests' then governance comes out well on top (ahead of strategy, organisational behaviour, finance, innovation, etc.).

'Governance' (if you are a cat) might feel like 'what those guys up there do' which is mostly…

> *Listening – to management, staff, external stakeholders, etc. – and reacting, offering counsel, challenging and giving or withholding support for major decisions. Maybe one per cent of what a Board (or Executive Committee) actually does is being proactive, most notably in the appointment (or renewal, or termination) of the Chief Executive Officer.*

Typically, as the organisation's 'highest authority', it is the Board, the Executive Committee or their equivalent, that oversees and orchestrates governance. Here the principles articulated previously, especially those emphasising the need to get the best Chair, are germane.

*One time, we (in management) just knew that the Chairman being mooted was the wrong call. This is dangerous territory but we persisted and got our point across. The alternative appointee did a brilliant job.*

In an organisation, the typical committee structures – for example, the Audit Committee, the Remuneration Committee, the Risk Committee, etc. – provide the mechanics of governance. In actual practice, good (or bad) governance pervades each and every level of business and is, like most of what we have been dealing with so far, very much dependent on specific people and their relationships with each other.

An issue which merits special mention in this regard is the nature of the relationship between the Chair and Chief Executive Officer in systems where these roles are separated.

*The Chair has to be both a mentor and a shoulder to cry on. But the Chair must also be strong enough to control the behaviour of protégés. Relationships between the executive team and the Board are always interesting.*

Good communication and trust-building 'upwards management' are, therefore, core skills of the cat herder and Chief Executive Officer in training. 'No surprises' is a good Golden Rule.

Another imperative is to keep a sense of perspective around values and ethics "when all about you seem to be losing theirs", sometimes no easy task in our highly competitive world, with ongoing pressure for 'results' – and, particularly, for bottom-line performance.

Confronted with almost daily examples of how badly people can behave in professional situations, it is necessary for you to role model ethical behaviour. A strong vision is needed at high level to marry the demands for short-term results with the long-term 'public good'.

> *Quality ethics is about marrying the short term with the long term. Whether it be pressure (temptation?) to manipulate accounts, or to turn a bit of a blind eye to pollution, instilling ethical behavior demands longer-term thinking.*
>
> *We need to ensure that short-term expediency is tempered by a clear view of long-term impacts. In the modern world, unethical behaviour will in due course be 'outed' and have repercussions.*
>
> *Back in 2002, around the celebrated judgement on the failed (Australian) insurer HIH Insurance Limited, Justice Owen sagely remarked: "I found myself rhetorically asking: did anyone stand back and ask themselves the simple question, is this right?"*

A very good question indeed.

## 7. Managing the CASH

*The ability to marshal financial resources is critical to success.*

When push comes to shove, there is good reason to conclude that leading and managing comes down to seeking organisational security, including, and primarily, financial security. For those in senior leadership, getting the finances right is a crucial matter.

And, as Mr Micawber so persuasively remarked in Charles Dickens's *David Copperfield*: "Annual income twenty pounds, annual expenditure nineteen pounds nineteen and six, result happiness. Annual income twenty pounds, annual expenditure twenty pounds ought and six, result misery."

**It's (always) a tough climate...** Close examination of the typical financial climate over past and present decades will show quite clearly that pressure on resources is the norm. The demands of development inevitably exceed the resources available, and therefore careful appraisal and management of those resources are required.

*There is never enough money – but there used to be.*

*"Do more with less." We hear this all the time.*

*It's a key management issue – businesses fail through a lack of cash. Cash is crucial for investment.*

So while (often expensive) equipment and talented people are undoubtedly central to progress, Lord Rutherford's wisdom remains germane: "We don't have all the resources we need, therefore we have to think."

**Cutting back...** Managing resources means not only the evaluation of the relative merits of different programmes and initiatives but also that choices need to be made. As we emphasise later on, meaningful strategy normally demands a reallocation of resources.

*Whatever the problem, equal misery for all is very rarely the right answer.*

*When it comes to making difficult choices… it is made more difficult when, from time to time, successful projects and/ or people have to be cut back to allow the resources to be available for the extraordinary opportunity.*

Some programmes will, therefore, need to contract, others to expand; new programmes will need to be created. This should be a process informed by the strategic direction of the organisation. Making the choices is not the most difficult part; the difficult issues are those associated with explaining and implementing such choices.

*When it comes to budget cuts, starting new programmes is easy; terminating old programmes is hard.*

How often have we not seen the proverbial 'hobby horse'? – the champions of the "tomorrow, just you wait and see" programme making the case for continuing after ten or more years without achieving a real outcome. But this horse has got two broken legs, it has gone blind, and all its hair is falling out. It needs a ceremonial (and urgent) shooting. Not easy, unless you can persuade the riders, who may not be in the it's-time-to-move-on category: "Here is this wonderful new horse and we need your riding skills…" Switching from a favoured domain to take up new challenges is seen by many to be fraught with difficulty.

> *It's always much easier – and ultimately very much more successful – to pull people than push them, especially where you've had past wins, but you're into diminishing returns. Set up an attractive place where they can see themselves, declare success (and don't say 'it's not sensible that we're still doing this'!). Then move on.*

**Your (personal) skill set…** If it is accepted that all professional environments have, at their core, vital issues of resourcing, then it should also be accepted that the effective leader and manager will need to be financially literate. In some professions this is the essence of the business, but not in all. Thus, when you come into a senior post, it is essential to acquire the necessary skills as a matter of some urgency if you do not already have them. This does not mean that you need to qualify hurriedly as a fully skilled management accountant on the side, but you must be able to read and easily understand sets of accounts, balance sheets, and so on, and to comment sensibly – particularly in debates with colleagues who may feel that they know far more than you do.

> *It's amazing how many people think they understand finance, and our finances. And they find it very easy to spend other people's money.*

While there are some dangers, in this area, of being too dependent on the experts, this concern should not prevent you from ensuring that you have highly skilled professional support when you need it. Indeed, one of the valuable assets of most professional partnerships is the range of in-house expertise that is on tap.

**Getting good help...** In this whole domain of finance there is one crucial piece of advice – and we give it based on some bad (and some good) experiences. Get at the top the VERY BEST financial person that you can possibly find and afford: a (much) broader thinker than the average number cruncher; interested in the wider organisation and in people; and someone with good communication skills. It is significantly beneficial to both you and your colleagues to have, as part of the team, an expert who is committed to the demystification of financial matters.

*Get to know and learn how to get help from smart finance people. Specifically... never ask for money... always ask for advice. If they give you advice... then they have bought into your project... and, sometimes, financial support follows... after all, it is now their project too!*

**The importance of elbow room...** Access to discretionary funding is important since it provides the leader with the ability to respond quickly to proposals that, in his or her judgement, warrant immediate support. The size of the discretionary, developmental fund is not as important as its existence (although it must be sufficient to enable real things to be achieved). It should be consistent with the organisation's strategy and used always in a disciplined way and, in the best-regulated organisations, it should be associated with overall financial security.

*Since money is probably your most important, and perhaps only, tool (e.g. for introducing change)... you need financial discipline to create the necessary margins.*

*If you don't get the money right, you can't do anything; if you do, then you can always do something.*

## GETTING THE JOB DONE – In Conclusion

As a leader, your job is to get results. First off, therefore, you had best make sure that there is crystal clarity as to what constitutes success – to and from those 'above', as well as down to those 'below'. If you don't achieve this, severe differences of opinion are inevitable down the track. In addition, the clarity you achieve will help you define your goals. Opaqueness and complexity can give rise to real problems here. On this journey, small wins – and celebrating them with those responsible – are helpful… Preparation is important, but so is fast on-the-job learning. Get away from your office whenever possible. Listen hard – across and up and down your organisation and, most particularly, listen to your key external stakeholders, especially your clients. Make sure you know those that can harm you, and those that can help you. And work hard at building relationships, and trust.

Consult, therefore, but accept that there must be limits. Be decisive. As far as possible be evidence-based, but trust your intuition. Plan well, but be tactically flexible around ways of reaching your strategic goals.

Delegate, where you have trust, and… more than you might think wise. But take care to ensure both role-clarity and goal-clarity (who's going to do what, and by when). But don't abdicate or even step back from your responsibilities: follow up, and follow through, including being meticulous over the necessary details. 'Execution excellence' is a hallmark of successful leaders.

Think twice (three times, four times?) before pulling the lever of organisational structural change.

Like salt, use committees sparingly, when you have to. Tight script, tight paperwork (in and out), with support from the best Chair you can find.

Finally, you may have a great strategy and be wonderfully skilled with your people, but resources, or rather lack of them, can bring you down. Money still makes the world go round. And you will never have enough of it. Also, at the end of the day, money is probably your only real tool for getting the changes you want implemented. If you don't speak the 'language', learn to converse, fast. And make sure you have those with top finance skills at your shoulder.

## C: MANAGING THE PEOPLE

While those in professional services are usually not uncomfortable in regarding themselves as 'business people', public sector professionals and academics often object to being considered part of a 'business', irrespective of the fact that they may be working in organisations which approach – or exceed – billion-dollar enterprises. Whatever the perspective, however, we believe that the perennial maxim "All business is people business" applies.

Thus, by design, this part of the book is the longest. It is also central. In it we seek to address the key issues germane to the recruitment, retention, deployment and motivation of your people.

We are convinced of the importance of talent in achieving success. In this section we address, *inter alia*, key traits of your talent pool – excellence, enthusiasm, judgement; the trials and tribulations of picking people, and, sometimes, having to let them go; and developing your people, managing performance and building your team.

We also deal with the priority that must be given to communication – the root of many problems, when it is done badly. Nevertheless, as one of our colleagues rightly labels it, it is '*the* baton' of leadership.

Finally, we emphasise the grossly underutilised weapon – in your 'talent war' armoury – of recognition, of giving credit where it is due, both formally and informally. And the consequences of doing it poorly, or unfairly.

All business is people business. Read on.


## 8. COLLEAGUES not subordinates ("It's all about the people")

In Section 4 we dipped into 'people and your time'. And its dominance thereon, because…

## C: MANAGING THE PEOPLE

*In the long run it's all about the talent.*

The effective management of your people – recruitment, development, deployment, motivation and retention – and your 'talent pipeline', is your single most important (and probably only) sustainable advantage. Next to getting the strategy right, it must therefore be your number one management priority.

*This is military campaign stuff – we truly are in a talent 'war'.*

Thus, keep your eye (and focus) on this very important ball...

*We were spending so much time on the detail around budgets, trying to get them to balance. Meanwhile good people were leaving.*

*The challenge of keeping our best talent is all-encompassing for us. There are so many great opportunities around the world.*

**Unleashing potential...** It is not enough just to have talent in your organisation, you need to nurture the conditions in which that talent can thrive.

"You can't motivate people. That door is locked from the inside. You can, however, create a climate in which most of your people will motivate themselves to help the organisation to reach its objectives." Robert Townsend (1920–98)

*Provide care, and context. Unleash, stop constraining. You'll get linear improvement in performance.*

In contrast...

*What brings out the worst in people? – insecurity, internal politics and misaligned ambition.*

More than a decade ago, taking a walk in a park, one of us saw an interesting (and all too rare) sign: "Please Walk on the Grass". Quite a surprise – and difference – from the normal "Don't" instruction; a tangible reminder of the essence of what good leadership is all about – the art of unlocking and exploiting the 'can do'. People can be like rubber bands – they have this wonderful capacity for stretch – if only we provide the pull, and the opportunities. Leadership at all levels – upwards and sideways, as well as just 'downwards' – is all about creating an environment where people can be the best they can possibly be.

*Inspirational leadership empowers people. It gets them excited and passionate about their work.*

*My job as a leader is to ignite and sustain the passion of others – and figure out how to do that in a professional situation where lots of the people are introverted to some degree.*

## In pursuit of excellence...

*The key thing about herding cats successfully is to have top quality cats.*

Having good people is *the* important step to operational success in an organisation, delivering the goals you have set, to the highest standard you can, across all aspects of the business you are in. So you need to have on your team the best people you can find:

"The people with the best people win." Jerry C. Welch (1948– ), innovative marketing executive.

*We target the best guys around the world and then make it easy and attractive for them to spend time with us.*

*Recruit the best and make it clear that excellence is the prime requirement.*

*'Talent attracts talent.' Get an outstanding individual on board, in a particular area, and other high achievers will join, seeking the chance to work with (or continue working with) the 'star'.*

There was, a while back, a radio interview with management expert Charles Handy, in which he talked about strategy and success. He told of a discussion with a senior school headmaster, reported to be 'the best of the best'. This man's secret, evidently, was along the lines of "It's easy. All I did was appoint the best Heads of Houses, and the best Heads of Department I could find, and then got out of the way. And waited five years."

It's not always quite that easy – (just) hiring 'good guys and letting them do whatever they want' is certainly no success guarantee, and may indeed lead to real problems. Handy rightly, therefore, went on to talk about the overarching importance of a sound 'framing' strategy (see Section 11) in which good people can excel; getting the culture, systems and organisational environment right is also important. But there's real wisdom in the headmaster's observation about the criticality of good people.

So how do we know what – or, rather, who – is good? The answer does not come without endeavour: it is absolutely necessary to do your homework and observe – as you'll know. Track record is always a pretty sound indicator of future performance. Then make sure you access reports first hand – not just formal referees' reports from former 'bosses' or supervisors, but also perspectives from well-respected peers, colleagues, subordinates. Also ask yourself: is the person an enthusiastic spirit? And – importantly – can he or she ignite that enthusiasm in others? Finally, are there clear signs that the goals you seek are going to be delivered? Some intelligent, articulate, passionate enthusiasts are closet non-deliverers – which a careful assessment of track record, sometimes 'reading between the lines' of written or verbal feedback, will hopefully (but, regrettably, not always) uncover.

**The secret of success?...** In order to foster success and achieve excellence it is critical to be aware of the underlying elements that are essential in reaching those goals. Many argue very persuasively that personal drive and single-mindedness are critical characteristics.

> "The average person puts only 25 percent of his energy and ability into his work. The world takes off its hat to those who put in more than 50 percent of their capacity, and stands on its head for those few and far between souls who devote 100 percent." Andrew Carnegie (1835–1919)

> *Finding and keeping the passion is the biggest role you can play as a leader.*

> "The real secret of success is enthusiasm. You can do anything if you have enthusiasm. Enthusiasm is the yeast that makes your hope rise to the stars. Enthusiasm is the sparkle in your eye, it is the swing in your gait, the grip of your hand, the irresistible surge of your will and your energy to execute your ideas. Enthusiasts are fighters. They have fortitude, they have staying qualities. Enthusiasm is at the bottom of all progress. With it there is accomplishment. Without it there are only alibis." Walter Chrysler (1875–1940)

> "The key is to keep company only with people who uplift you, whose presence calls forth your best." Chad Harbach (*The Art of Fielding*, 2012)

The world of the professions is replete with examples of intelligently-applied enthusiasm and focused drive overcoming great obstacles.

> "It's important to stay focused. I've learned that over the years – and it pays off in the end." Roger Federer (1981– ), tennis champion.

But also note by way of caution…

> *Because many workers involved with commissions from the public domain are passionate idealists, the personal is very often mixed in with the professional but the line needs to be*

*drawn, and navigated with care, to ensure the professional takes precedence.*

**Moving up...** When strong performers consistently produce quality outputs, it is necessary for that to be recognised. One natural form of recognition is advancement in the organisation. The skills needed in delivery are often those needed in leading and managing – the producers of today are the leaders of tomorrow. If this is you, here's some advice:

*If you trust the people you are working for, stay. If not, leave... If trust is positive both up and down, then be patient... because your superiors will want you to continue to be successful... and so you must wait until the right opportunity arises to move you up to a position of more responsibility that you can handle and become an evident (and so promotable) success.*

*Be brave... Say "Yes" to new challenges. If your boss has hopes for you, he or she will want to prepare you for later promotions.*

*Broaden your interests. The specialism in which you first established your reputation is not the only field of interest in the world. Spend time (like lunch breaks) with experts in other related fields.*

**Selecting people...** Next to getting the strategy right, this is probably the most important thing you will need to master as a leader.

*I would have valued knowing both how hard it is to hire the right person for the job and how critical it is to make the correct match. If you hire right, management is easier.*

*We are very careful in hiring new people. Thereafter our leadership role is to help them to be successful. We work very hard on this. If they don't make it, we feel bad.*

*The average staff member's career with us is about eleven years. Which means, when you're making an appointment,*

> *you are – on average – making a million-dollar plus decision, and that's the direct salary cost only. Compare and contrast the time and effort put into other million-dollar decisions and you'll find many appointment processes are seriously underdone.*

Getting a good 'hit rate' in making staff appointments is imperative. Getting a variety of different inputs and perspectives – internally and externally – from peers, those more senior and those more junior, can be very valuable in helping you make the decision. There's a great moment in the film *Dead Poets Society* where the school teacher, Mr Keating (played by Robin Williams), jumps up onto a desk and makes a point, to his class, on the importance of getting a different perspective – "Up here, I look different to you; down there, you look different to me." Thus, engaging a variety of people in the selection process can provide valuable insight around those people themselves. This can all be time-consuming, but almost invariably it is well worth the effort.

> *For senior appointments we ran three (advisory to me) selection committees, each interviewing all shortlisted candidates – bosses plus some peers; subordinates; and (external) stakeholders. Rarely did they reach the same conclusion. But the wealth of insight and differing perspectives greatly improved the chances of getting the decision right. We borrowed the idea from Hewlett-Packard, I seem to remember.*

> *By running appointment committees myself, not only am I in charge of a critical appointment, but I learn a lot about the people on the committee.*

Be very clear about who owns the appointment: committee(s) don't, nor does your HR department; ownership is your responsibility. On those occasions when an appointment doesn't work out, people will run for cover.

> *I've never used a truly democratic process for finally appointing members of my immediate team. I'm the one on*

*the line, since I have to work with them on a day-to-day basis and I'm ultimately responsible for the results we achieve.*

And, as mentioned above, the real support and mentoring work starts the day the new member of staff accepts appointment.

Two important last words in the selection/hiring game:

One – no matter what the urgency, it is always better not to appoint than to appoint the wrong person. Often this means resisting pressure from others who see (and frequently exaggerate) the problems associated with delay.

*Never appoint a weak appointee.*

Two – when hiring into your professional organisation, you're frequently in long-term relationship building. For example:

*When you take on a new graduate, very often you're taking on a relationship for well beyond the time you actually work together.*

Personal relationships are vital in all that we do, and can be revisited with interest a surprising number of decades later.

**On stretch...** People have great capacity for stretch. And this can – and should – be cascaded 'down' through each level in the organisation.

*When you stretch your people, and tell them that they are capable of doing far more than they think they can, they do perform and indeed can outperform their own concept of themselves.*

*There's no doubt that encouragement and persuasion work best. But people don't just need praise, they need to believe that you think that they have the skills to do even better.*

**Qualification(s)...** Three points here. One – qualifications are a guide not a rule book. Two – 'credentials' go way beyond the paper qualifications. Three – due diligence pays. Always double check that you're getting what you think you're getting.

Competition for jobs can do funny things to people, particularly in hard times. There are, sadly, far too many examples of appointments being based on misinformation.

**The diversity challenge, and the 'affirmative action' paradox...** There is, necessarily, a significant emphasis placed on equal opportunities and related legislation in the prevailing employment climate. This means that great care must be given to ensuring that all the procedures up to any final selection meet the required standards. But this can occasionally allow paradoxical issues to surface. When does a manifest commitment to equality of opportunity become 'affirmative action'? The former is a legal requirement, the latter is not. It is important that this difference is both recognised and understood.

> *Always make the best appointment – not the 'almost best' because of other influences or pressures.*

Yet...

> *It was amazing to see how the diversity in our leadership team improved the richness of our discussions, and the quality of our decision-taking.*

> *There is no doubt that a more evenly balanced leadership team is an attraction for female talent.*

> *We just weren't getting female applicants for our middle tier appointments. Evidently they thought they wouldn't stand much chance. So we ran a 'women only' round, weathered the outrage, and got a really good number of quality applications. We made three outstanding appointments.*

> *The business case for more female appointments was clear – we were losing talent. No quick fix, but more role models appointed and getting the 'pipeline' (supply-side) flowing has got us moving.*

At the end of the day, the lifeblood of all professional organisations is ideas, and...

"Where do new ideas come from? That's simple. From differences. The best way to maximise differences is to mix ages, culture, disciplines. Hire diversity." Nicholas Negroponte (1943– ), American architect and founder of the M.I.T. Media Lab.

**New brooms versus old brooms?...** Often there are very good reasons to bring in the 'new broom'. But – like Love, as in the song Love is All Around – most organisations of our type are also brimming with talent, ready to take on new challenges and opportunities.

> "I use the rule of 50 per cent. Try to find somebody inside your organisation with a record of success and an appetite for the job. If he or she looks like 50 per cent of what you need, give them the job. In six months they'll have grown the other 50 per cent – and everybody will be satisfied." Robert Townsend (1920–1998)

**On judgement...** Along with enthusiasm and track record, sound judgement can be a most important attribute in choosing and promoting staff.

*When it comes to people, if there's one key word it's 'judgement' – the ability to assess the situation, give the best advice and take the best course of action.*

Here, as in making quality decisions (see Section 4), intuition plays a part. Judgement is not something that can be taught. If it is to be learned at all, it is learned through observation and experience. Once gained, it is a great asset.

*To lead successfully you need to have developed a track record such that people trust your judgement.*

Another paradox here is illustrated through the old story around making quality judgements: "Q: How do you make good decisions? A: Through experience. Q: But how do you get experience? A: Through making bad decisions."

*You can teach the detailed technical leadership, but you can't teach the bigger picture stuff; it's an experience thing. And some have the ability, and some find it difficult.*

**Building the team...** The necessity is to harness both individualism and the strength of the team:

> "Many of the best ideas, concepts, and innovations come from a single person's insight. You get these amazing bits of work from inspired individuals who have the freedom to act, when they have the tools and knowledge they need. But to scale any operation takes the work of teams, and, more often than not, teams of teams. Leaders inspire that flash of genius and also make those individuals want to work together. Great teamwork is a real skill. Finding a way to nurture individual passion and pride while at the same time creating a spirit of teamwork is a hallmark of the leaders I admire most. Pulling off both of those in the same organization is magical but essential." Mark Shuttleworth (1973– ), IT entrepreneur and the world's second self-funded space tourist.

*The role of leaders... in a global world is now almost too big and difficult for any one individual. We look for heroes, but true leadership is now in teams.*

There is a lot of very good information available about teams, and about the demands of building them and leading them effectively. There are also useful tools, such as the Myers-Briggs Type Indicator and the Belbin Team Role Inventory, for gaining better understanding of individuals and of how they see their roles in teams.

*Never underestimate the power of positive camaraderie in the senior leadership team. When they all believe in the vision and mission and strategy, the people hear the same message, although it may be expressed differently.*

## C: MANAGING THE PEOPLE

> *I gained a lot by using a consultant to find out what I needed to know about teams and their collective merits.*

Carefully planned, and very carefully managed, 'breakaway' sessions can also be useful when designed to complement 'on the job' learning. Five-star, objective, facilitation is fundamentally important – a 'make or break' imperative. Here your detailed spadework in facilitator selection is the order of the day.

> *I needed earlier to know that it is critically important to have a strong management team.*
>
> *I underestimated how long it would take to change the culture of the senior management group towards my way of working, and away from that of my predecessor.*
>
> *For transformation you often need first to transform the management team.*

But in making the transformations it is important to avoid setting up, deliberately or inadvertently, what might be seen as an 'inner' group:

> *Beware the 'Kitchen Cabinet'. Don't have an A-team and a B-team. You usually have some very good people who deliver quality, quickly; and others less so. But always favouring A-players with tough, stretching assignments builds up the pressure on them, and resentment of those they see not working so hard. Resentment on both sides, in fact, as the B-players may well feel that they are regarded as 'outsiders'. Your leadership job is also to build the skills of the B-players on your team.*

The time and effort you spend with – and developing – your team needs to be appropriately balanced with quality, one-on-one time spent with your individual team members – and all done of course in the context of the objectives you are seeking to achieve. Simply put, it is all about the 'three-legged stool' balancing act of leadership: task–team–individual.

> *Too often, especially under pressure, the whole focus is on getting the job done, 'whatever it takes'. Regrettably, when we are not careful, 'it' can detract from the team-building and individual-growing responsibilities which are key to balanced leadership.*

Then 'task' has become all, and it's like a stool with only one, fat, long leg – unstable, and not sustainable.

**Developing the talent...** Visible and tangible commitment from, and engagement with, top management is a key to the success of leadership development programmes – helping colleagues develop their skills both in their current roles and in preparation for roles to come. If development processes are simply routine activities, run out of the 'Human Resources' department, then a lack of commitment is more than likely. Certainly bringing on younger colleagues should be a top priority for the leader.

> *Leadership development is critical for our future. We need to put in substantially more effort here. It's probably the chief executive's only sustainable legacy.*

> *If I had my time again I would devote three times as much time and resources to nurturing our leadership development programs.*

> *The most important test of a successful leader is, in my view, the extent to which he or she has contributed to the development of the leadership capability of others, across many levels within the institution.*

So as leaders we're in the people-growing business. There's a Chinese proverb which states, around wealth: "If you want a year of wealth, grow grain; if you want ten years of wealth, grow trees; if you want a hundred years of wealth, grow people."

> "The conductor doesn't make a sound. The conductor's power depends on his ability to make other people

powerful." Benjamin Zander (1939– ), Conductor and Music Director of the Boston Philharmonic Youth Orchestra.

**Caring for the talent (and everybody else)...** There are also other, more domestic, aspects of dealing with your staff that should not be overlooked. More is required than just giving attention to the mechanics of management. Good leaders and managers also have a human face which can show in a variety of ways – such as concern about matters outside the workplace or an awareness of important health and family issues. Of course, this must be tempered by care about intrusion on privacy. Experience shows that different staff respond to different overtures in different ways. Nevertheless, there is merit in making it clear that there is a sense of caring in the organisation.

*Strongly promoting workplace safety, and staff health – even 'bike to work' programmes, or 'fruit and nuts not biscuits' at tea-times – says we care about your health in your place of work and, therefore, we care about you.*

**And that includes 'Supporters' Club' members...** While an army (reportedly) marches on its stomach – and your 'soldiers' (the specialist professionals) are the front-liners – all professional organisations are operationally very dependent on the quality and efficiency of their 'support' staff – even though they don't necessarily always realise it. The care and attention given to senior staff and colleagues must be balanced by an awareness of the needs of others in the organisation since they are also prominent ambassadors 'around town', and a litmus test for organisational health.

*It's good to stay in touch with the janitors and secretarial and support staff. They often know a lot more about what's going on and where the issues and problems are than your senior staff do!*

'Signs and symbols' – of inclusivity and equality – are often closely examined as indicators of a leader's commitment (or otherwise) to parity of esteem and opportunity:

> *I tried always to find ways to make it very clear that our support staff were very important – visibility and senior level representation on promotions committees – and even down to equality of car parking – the latter not without some contention, I might add!*

**And on the topic of Incentives and Motivation…** This can be a difficult area. There are many alternative ways of providing incentives. It is necessary to think (significantly) beyond simple financial rewards:

> *It is important to try to understand what motivates people. Our type of environment is different from 'normal' business life, and you can't work it out in one meeting. And the motivators can be very different – personal (financial) reward is rarely the driver. For example… Mr A is a great host, facilitates workshops and conferences, and makes people welcome – he has built a global family and keeping it in touch and harmonious is his prime driver. Personal prestige is Ms B's key motivator – the awards she gets, the media appearances – it is all about recognition, and looking good. Dr C, the easiest to deal with, is motivated by remuneration (and, in particular, how he's doing relative to others). Mrs D is motivated by seeing her staff do well – she enjoys being 'the back for them to climb on'. Mr E is solely and obsessively motivated by the intellectual.*

In the motivation stakes, in a cats culture, titles, too, can be important:

> *Even though they all say they don't respect hierarchy the label on their door can mean a lot to them.*

If you know what the primary personal drivers are, you can better craft the incentive structures to support optimal performance.

*What motivates people? Power and recognition and financial reward, and giving them the space, time and freedom where they can take the credit.*

*Opportunities and encouragement to innovate bring out the best in people. The ability to fly with something that catches their eye will keep cats happy and energised.*

*The management of creative professionals starts and ends with encouraging, supporting and incentivising achievement.*

*Incentivisation has to reflect the longer-term nature of partnerships and the custodianship felt by generations of partners. This is not a short-term game.*

**But about remuneration...** The pay cheque, we are often told, is a second-order priority for individuals who choose a career in the professions – particularly in public service, the not-for-profit sector and academia. This may be so, but it is an increasingly important competitive component in the talent attraction and retention stakes. And it's too important for you not to be reasonably hands-on in the process. We are not (yet) into professional footballer type trading but top talent can certainly negotiate hard.

And while, in an ideal world, the 'tea room wall test' should apply – total packages, including bonuses, displayed from highest to lowest like exam results – confidentiality considerations and restrictions generally make this a hard thing to do in practice. The 'workers in the vineyard' parable (Matthew 20: 1–16) would also undoubtedly click in – people previously 'happy' with their pay would become instantly unhappy when they saw, without any explanation, what some others got. Suffice it to say that, in any decision-making situation, you should have the (theoretical) tea room wall test in mind, and be able to justify each and every decision, hand on heart.

## Managing performance...

> *You need to be honest with people. Straight with them. Sometimes it's very hard. Good people welcome an honest appraisal of how they're doing.*

> *Whenever I mentor a new manager and potential leader my number one piece of advice is 'be as honest as possible'... Trust builds a strong team and is essential for them to believe in that vision.*

Dr Rod Eddington, a former CEO of British Airways, remembers back to when he was Deputy CEO of Cathay Pacific Airways. The management team took on the task of improving skills across the whole organisation in giving and receiving day-to-day feedback. It proved essential when it came to holding people accountable and managing for good performance, but it was an arduous undertaking. While 'feedback is the food of champions' – it is how we all improve and grow – giving feedback is often hard to do, and even harder to do well. Get some coaching, experiment through role-playing – practice and more practice – it is a never-ending journey.

> *I would have benefited from more strategic leadership and mentoring on performance management right from the start.*

> *Professional organisations built around specialist expertise are often not very good at performance management, and the more senior the member of staff, the harder it is to deal with underperformance.*

And for getting off on the right foot, like the 'catch them doing things right' advice we were given while raising our children...

> *Before getting to what you want achieved, start with praise and not what's wrong with the current arrangements. If you start with what's wrong, usually people don't hear the way forward.*

Getting really good at managing performance is a skill worth acquiring:

*Around feedback, one great boss I had was a genius. I would go in for a chat, get a clear message where improvement was needed, but come out feeling good about myself and about our relationship, and fired up.*

*With good leaders people learn. They create the playing field for success.*

*The best bosses I've had help you see something in yourself you haven't seen. They are adaptive to different styles and create the dialogue that allows learning to occur, and they empower their people to make choices, and to grow, providing a safety net to do so. You walk out with insight, not feeling beaten up.*

Overall, therefore, it is the day-to-day assessments that are key and necessary for the good manager's armoury. But 'formal' performance appraisals (e.g. yearly) often have questionable value, especially as they can make an artificial short-term event out of a continuing responsibility. And at the end of the day, again…

*What do I look for from my boss? Consistency and honesty – both when I've done well and when I've messed up.*

**Organising the team…** Structure is the handmaiden of talent management and strategy – not vice versa. But there is a paradox here. On the one hand, deciding 'who you want on your bus' is a priority. Flexible structures (and titles) can facilitate the recruitment and retention of talented performers, and should be used as such – taking into account the potential unintended consequences and perceived precedent-setting that may arise. Conversely, compromising your own organisational design principles (and probably confusing the rest of your organisation) to move individuals sideways rather than moving them 'out' is invariably a mistake.

**Letting them go: the trials and tribulations of termination…**
This is an area of activity that more often than not makes people uncomfortable. But it is part of the territory of leading and managing. It is certain that, as a new leader, you will, surprisingly early on, encounter the situation where one of the team you have inherited (or someone you have hired) either is identified as not having the skills expected or just does not fit in with the new ethos. And they may have to go.

> *I wish, in my earlier career, that I'd spent more time learning about leadership which might have mitigated my two biggest management faults: lack of clarity about where I wanted to take the organisation, and lack of decisiveness in dispensing with inadequate people.*

Most often, here, we are not talking about issues of gross incompetence, financial irregularity or inappropriate behaviour, but rather the simple manifestation of the 'Peter Principle'. The sooner you acknowledge that 'this isn't working' the better. Again this is a place to trust your intuition in taking the first steps. And determining an effective way forward is then the order of the day. Providing timely, honest, unambiguous feedback is critical – delayed, mixed messages just muddy the water…

> *You're not doing anyone a favour by keeping him or her on in a job they're not up to. It's not kind to be kind – it's cruel to be kind.*

Re-defining or re-scoping the non-achiever's job, for example by reducing their span of responsibility, can work on some occasions, particularly where you yourself have been responsible for creating a 'mission impossible' job, or have perhaps overvalued a person's strengths and talent. But this is seldom the best solution.

> *It is hard getting rid of people, and I've never been very good at it.*

Because it is so hard, letting a colleague go can become more painful than it needs to be. And only rarely will your task be made easier by the person involved 'falling on their sword'. Also, because all action must conform with the legal frameworks within which the organisation operates, leaders can worry about legal comebacks, get officious and behave insensitively or even abnormally. 'Do as you would be done by' is a good guideline.

*In the purely commercial world there is greater emphasis on being successful, and somewhat less on being compassionate. You need to be sure to emphasise both.*

So your target should become one of seeking to help the individual, using care and investing time and support – and generosity (not necessarily financial generosity) – in identifying separation possibilities, including the prospect of moving on to a next assignment, probably outside the organisation. More often than not the individual concerned ends up happier too (though maybe not in the first instance).

*I have often been surprised by how many 'failing' colleagues have known deep down that they are proverbial square pegs in round holes.*

The trick is to find a way, as far as possible, to help a colleague save face and maintain his or her self-esteem without inadvertently compromising your own values or credibility or business objectives. How, when, and what you – together – communicate therefore makes a huge difference.

In the challenge of termination, there are also two notable 'Bewares'.

Number 1: The Two-Year Rule

*Over a twenty-year period we observed that it was typically two years (at least) from when we (or I) first observed 'smoke under the door' to the point when the person concerned left that job, or the organisation. Ouch!*

> *Deferring a decision because "He's only got 18 months to run on his contract" can be a mistake. A lot of damage can be done in 18 months.*

Number 2: "But They're So Difficult"

> *You can't fire people for being difficult. Most organisations have their share of rather difficult people, but our type of organisation is often stacked with them. I've seen difficult (but clever and competent) people be a 'burr under the saddle' for a decade. You have to accept it and manage around them.*

Perversely, of course, it is also important to remember that 'difficult people' are often the source of some of your success:

> "Business needs a massive transfusion of talent; and talent, I believe, is most likely to be found among non-conformists, dissenters and rebels." David Ogilvy (1911–1999)

Finally, one of the most intractable challenges in the 'cats' environment is re-motivating, or moving out, the borderline performer:

> *This is one of the toughest problems we have. I struggle with the 'coasters': they're not terrible. But they just don't deliver what you'd hoped for – and the excuses are usually just about believable. I have no good answers here. You just have to get more Machiavellian.*

But maybe they are just being measured by the wrong yardstick. Maybe there's a 'vein of gold' buried inside that you have to work harder at finding. Changing the goalposts – if you can – could then be a quick and effective fix. In other cases, you can try loading them with 'dog work' (that they'll probably also do poorly). You can starve them of resources. You can give them time off, and away, to re-invent themselves (and, perhaps, to look for a job elsewhere). You can bite the bullet, and buy them out – although this is usually best only as a last resort, unless there is real urgency. And you can have (time-consuming, and sometimes frustrating) 'deep and meaningful' dialogues to seek to identify a mutually beneficial way forward. But all in all, it is never easy and never without pain.

On the brighter side, such processes can, with the benefit of hindsight, become opportunities for improving your hiring practices.

**Disciplinary action...** This is best avoided – if you can avoid it without compromising your principles, or those of the organisation. This is a last resort, and there are no winners. The only real exception is when the law has been broken – then it is necessary to act quickly and firmly.

**And don't forget your external Supporters' Club...** With the exception of those (generally very few) staff who have left under the proverbial cloud, most of your past staff members, especially those who have retired after long and loyal service, will almost certainly feel good about the organisation and want it to succeed into the future. Your alumni are therefore an important part of your PR machine. And a free – and usually relatively untapped – source of experience and wisdom. Resource them, and keep them informed.

**A final reminder (and lest we forget)...**

*All business is people business. Full stop.*

## 9. COMMUNICATION, COMMUNICATION, COMMUNICATION

No matter how hard you try, the most consistent complaint will be about poor communication... you should accept the criticism and try harder still... never stop trying to communicate better.

*Communication? We never do enough.*

John O'Neil, who runs the Centre for Leadership Renewal in San Francisco, calls communication excellence 'the baton of leadership'. We agree. Six quick points of elaboration:

**A daily problem...** If you look, objectively, at the disasters (big or small) that you've observed in the past, both in your organisation and elsewhere, a high percentage might be laid – in part or in whole – at the door of inter-person communication problems.

There's the well-known (even hackneyed) – but perhaps not sufficiently taken to heart – World War I story: the Major and his troops are in the trenches, up to their ears in mud and blood, wanting to move. Communications are down; he sends a message "Send reinforcements, we're going to advance." A couple of miles back, with the verbal message having been passed on a couple of times, the general in charge hears "Send three and four pence; we're going to a dance." How often have you seen this kind of mis-communication? Enough said...

*Not communicating clearly... brings out the worst in people.*

*He may have had good reasons for what he did, but these were not perceived by those expected to work with the results. Uncommunicated intentions mean very little.*

*Person-to-person and person-to-people communication stuff-ups cost our organisation heaps in terms of lost time, unnecessary re-work, demotivation and upset. Ah – if I had but one wish from a lady with a magic wand...!*

**Communication and change...** Much leadership time is taken up in the effective management of change. Reflecting on a major study (by Prosci, USA) of many organisations in states of change – effective and otherwise – it is clear that well-conducted and well-managed communication is a dominant factor in successfully implementing change.

> *If you have a vision and you expect your people to run with it, but they don't properly understand it, you're probably going to fail.*
>
> "Stop nuancing. Simple, clear messages get through." John McTernan (Communications Director for Australian Prime Minister, Julia Gillard)

In any change process, you need to be crystal clear – in your own mind, to your team, and to the organisation – about the direction in which you're headed:

> *You must, repeat must, keep your strategic messages very clear: very straightforward, easily understood and digestible – simple terms, easy to remember and to understand, and to pass on. And then repeat, repeat, repeat. Be boring.*
>
> *Sometimes you seem to need to repeat things at least seven times and then people begin to understand!*

**Listening skills…** Communication is two-way and, as Stephen Covey wisely observed, "Seek first to understand, then to be understood."

> *Most leaders talk too much… it's an occupational hazard.*
>
> *Even in a senior and sophisticated management group you can never assume that what is being heard by a set of ears is that which comes out of a particular mouth.*
>
> *You need to develop ways to check that your communication is effective (do not assume it is and do not assume repetition will make it more so) – listening to something meaningful can be a strength of 'cats' – hearing is not the same thing.*
>
> *You know when they are really listening, as opposed to thinking about the next point they want to make. Good leaders help people in active listening – to be both emotionally as well as physically present.*

And for you as a leader, the old maxim, previously mentioned, that 'feedback is the food of champions' definitely applies.

Indeed, you should be going out of your way to be seen as something of a role model – to make it easy and non-threatening for your colleagues to comment when they see you falling short…

So it's imperative to listen to criticisms from the team and really pay attention. It takes guts to tell a senior executive they are making mistakes, and even if only a couple tell you, probably lots of others are thinking the same.

> *We have robust conversations in a respectful way. We track the outcomes of those conversations, and then operationalise them.*

> *It was tough moving into a leadership position where virtually everybody was older than me. Some, a lot so. I quickly learned to watch my words, listen, learn from them.*

But regrettably…

> *Sometimes, extremely capable leaders just stop listening. They get weak people around them and get stuck, and become enamoured with their own ability. Eventually they self-destruct.*

## The personal touch…

> *The more you can achieve personal contact, with frank and honest communication, the better.*

> *People want to know what's going on, and want to hear it directly from the leader. Even if they don't like what they hear.*

And adults like stories, just as children like stories. Especially those stories with a personal, experiential flavour:

> *Stories are very important in communication.*

> *Stories provide an emotional resonance. Better still if they've got a rational, analytic base.*

**Be creative...** Colleagues from Xerox tell the (perhaps apocryphal) story of staff complaining, in the common way: "They never tell us what's going on around here", while noting that if a juicy rumour is put into the organisation in twenty minutes everybody knows all about it! As a result they changed their communication processes to mirror more closely the way in which rumours get conveyed.

*So if you think your message 'from the top' will not be 'cascaded' accurately, timeously (or even at all), think again – get real, and creative.*

*Whether it's good news or bad, we always try to ensure that our staff members know it first, and don't first read about it in the newspapers or on the internet.*

**Actions versus words...**

*I communicate behaviours every day. Sometimes I even use words.*

Words are only a small percentage of the message. An illustrative anecdote: the gifted communicator Nelson Mandela preached reconciliation in creating a new South Africa from the schisms of apartheid. He also lived his words... He knew that rugby dominated the white man's sporting agenda in that nation. At the 1995 Rugby World Cup Final in Johannesburg, President Mandela came onto the ground to meet the teams, wearing a Number 6 Springbok jersey (a replica of that of the Springbok captain, Francois Pienaar). No words were spoken that the crowd could hear, but the very largely white audience in the stadium got the message, loud and clear. Many present had tears in their eyes. Actions can speak louder than words, so they say.

Relatedly, and in contrast, there's the old saying along the lines of "I can't hear what you're saying, because it's drowned out by what I see you doing."

> *If you are pronouncing values for your organisation, and at the same time you show your own behaviour is inconsistent and you are doing things that don't respect these values, you only fail once.*

**So, summarising 'the story so far'...** Communication issues often lead to (twice? thrice?) daily problems. 'Getting it right' – key to managing any successful change initiative (see also Section 12) – requires honing your listening skills (as opposed to your talking skills, which you probably do pretty well). It is very much enhanced by the personal touch and often requires creativity and imagination. What you do (as opposed to what you say) also generally communicates volumes.

We now move on, in this communication-related section, to some other thorny communication-related issues such as email, the media (social and otherwise), PowerPoint and annual reports...

**Beware the tyranny of the email...**

> *I was told that there are now close to 300 billion emails sent every day. That's 2.8 million every second. Or approximately 90 trillion each year. Happily some 80 per cent go straight to junk mail. Half of the rest seem to end up in my Inbox.*

The rise and rise of email is both a blessing and a potential problem. Instead of being a valuable aid to communication, emails can become both a consuming tyranny and a landscape fraught with danger. It is quite normal for the common courtesies of letters to be cast to the winds. It is surprising just how many times you see statements in emails that are ill-judged and intemperate in ways that were rare in old-fashioned handwritten correspondence.

Emails seem to engender a sense of urgency that can become quite out of proportion:

> *When my prime objective became clearing my inbox each day, I knew I had my priorities quite wrong.*

> *There is no difficult email (or letter) which cannot be improved by at least eight hours sleep.*
>
> *On email, nobody ever has the last word.*

If you are not careful, your words can also be used – often selectively, and out of context – against you.

> *Our environments tend to be pretty leaky. I ended up never crafting an email (except to my team, or other close colleagues etc.) without thinking through how it (or an extract) would come across on the front page of the local newspaper.*

If you're communicating something important by email, never assume that it has been read, and understood. "But I sent you an email!" is a very lame rebuke.

**But there is a place for the old-fashioned letter...** A useful rule – when you've got something nice to say, write a letter; where there's a problem, pick up the phone or, better still, if you can, go across for a chat. It is amazing how often people get this the wrong way round. Thus:

> *Communicating in writing when a face-to-face discussion is required usually brings out the worst in people.*

Both in you and in them.

**Mass messaging...** As a means of communication to many, email is not communication – it is broadcasting. Whether or not your mass email messages have been seen, understood and internalised is often very open to question.

> *'Global' emails (to all staff) are not often viewed positively by staff as a method of communication – too top-down, too impersonal, the voice 'from the top of the mountain'.*
>
> *As one of my top industry friends says, it's so nice and easy to send twenty thousand emails by pressing one button, but I've not yet worked out how to answer them all.*

To be realistic, however, when large numbers of staff need to be communicated with quickly and efficiently, email can be a boon. Thus, judicious and creative use of email can provide a solid means of information transfer and of keeping people in the picture. But these messages must usually be simple, short and clear. Draft them, and test them by seeking feedback on them from a colleague whose judgement you trust. Try hard to avoid typos: "Even the boss isn't into quality, so why should *I* bother?"

**Reply to your emails...**

> *What brings out the best in people? Engage with them. Respond to every email.*

It's usually a good idea to try to deal with your emails personally (and promptly) rather than have them vetted for you, since important messages can get missed. This doesn't mean you need to draft all the responses. It can be very efficient to look emails over and then send them on (with brief comments) to be handled, personally and timeously, by someone close to you whose judgement and finesse you value.

A simple but valuable stratagem for allaying the fears of colleagues that they are being ignored or overlooked, is to generate very basic responses along the lines of "Thank you for your message. I will get back to you shortly/by this afternoon/tomorrow/next week" – and then make sure you *do* that! This quick-shot reply can help to bring the temperature down and keep relationships intact.

> *With 300+ emails a day, I needed some prioritisation system. What works for me is automatic sorting to give me #1: from outside, addressed only to me; #2: from inside addressed only to me; #3: all emails addressed to me but as one of a number of recipients; #4: all where I'm just copied in, Cc or Bcc.*
>
> *Blind copying can be a problem. As well as clogging up my inbox, what do I do with information I'm not supposed to*

C: MANAGING THE PEOPLE

*have, apart from worry about it? A colleague banned all blind copying in his organisation, evidently to good effect.*

**Social media…** This is a comparatively new development in the workplace in all organisations but it is very clear that the available technologies – Twitter, Facebook, LinkedIn, blogs and more – are now very much a part of the landscape. They can have both positive and negative features.

In any event they need to be managed, and all organisations should be thinking – or already have thought – carefully about their policies for dealing with these technologies. Consideration of the possible impacts of various social media is significantly important: both in their roles as possible tools for people management and as challenges to people management.

"How do we get beyond e-mail to these new social platforms that include an industrial-strength social network? Not through Facebook, because that's not the right tool. But there are tools now: wikis, blogs, microblogging, jams, next-generation project management – what I call collaborative decision management. These are social tools for decision making. These are the new operating systems for the 21st-century enterprise in the sense that these are the platforms upon which talent works, and performs, and creates capability." Don Tapscott (1947– ) Canadian business executive, author and consultant.

What is important is to accept that they cannot just be left to look after themselves.

*I'm still getting my head around social media. Things can go viral very quickly, especially in combination, e.g. radio with social media. You've got to have a strong strategic communications plan, that articulates where social media fits in and continually monitors activities.*

> *Social media may bring big challenges – but it's also a wonderful feedback tool and can be used very effectively as such.*
>
> *Social networking provides a great opportunity to knowledge-share in professional service firms without hierarchy or barriers, but it has to be remembered that professionalism is needed in all forms of communication.*
>
> *How do we respond collectively to an environment where what's 'right' isn't determined by the law but by what's on Twitter?*

Then there is the time-wasting issue. It is generally accepted that in the recent past many employees spent much time playing various forms of Patience on their screens (when they thought no one was looking), but the lure of Facebook and its equivalents is far stronger. A recent newspaper article told of a man who has employed someone to sit near him in his office and hit him if he starts to log in to Facebook!

This area is so new that there are as yet no hard or fast rules – indeed the jury is hardly seated in judgement of how leaders should deal with these issues. But there is no doubt that social media are here to stay, and this means that their role must be engaged with, and dealing with them must be given careful thought.

**Dealing with the media...** We all know that the media are everywhere and that they operate with varying degrees of intrusiveness. All leaders need a well-thought-through policy for dealing with media approaches. As a general rule, when a journalist rings up, take the call – or at the very least, in order to get your head around the issues, respond with a "Give me ten minutes and I'll get back to you." And, again – make sure that you do. Within eight minutes would be better.

> *Journalists are often inherently lazy, and/or very busy and time-strapped. Feed them regularly and proactively.*

## C: MANAGING THE PEOPLE

*The media like to publish everything that is negative; but when you have something positive to tell often they're not interested.*

An enlightening observation from one journalist was, "Thank you very much for talking to me; it was very helpful. If you hadn't spoken to me, I'd have probably just made up a response."

*We once made the mistake of getting into an extremely confrontational relationship with a particular journalist. So much so that we eventually declined any contact, having been advised, "Don't give him any oxygen". This proved, in hindsight, to have been a serious error. He got his (well-polluted) 'oxygen' elsewhere. And we suffered from the 'power of the pen'.*

Excellent training courses, focused on dealing with the media, are now available. These are usually one-on-one for senior leaders. It is a brave leader who believes that he or she has no need for advice and guidance in this area.

*Media training is fundamentally important.*

**The Annual Report...** This is a necessary evil for which the cost-benefit ratio is probably very unfavourable. Minute attention to detail is usually required – so make sure someone on your team with the necessary obsessive instincts is in charge. But top leadership time allocated to the two- to three-page overview is, without doubt, a good investment. When published, the Annual Report can also be a useful, and motivational, information 'circular' for the rest of your organisation (and for key stakeholders, including alumni).

Take care to get the 'look and feel' right. And make copies available to everyone – it is surprising just how many people (from the 'top' to the 'bottom') like to take a copy home to show off to the family and friends: "This is where I work, and this is what we do. Pretty cool, eh?"

## Death by PowerPoint?...

*Power corrupts. PowerPoint corrupts absolutely.*

PowerPoint is not as intrusive as email and obviously has widespread and useful applications. But it can take on a life of its own and, in the process, create a serious dependency. In that context it is instructive to look at the spoof PowerPoint version of the Gettysburg Address (http://norvig.com/Gettysburg/) – something of a cold shower for those over-enthused with this form of 'communication'. And, interestingly, Apple founder and CEO Steve Jobs evidently banned it from being used in any meeting he attended.

*For a medium that has such a dominant influence on credibility and reputation, it is astounding how frequently PowerPoint presentations are undertaken so poorly.*

A rhetorical question: over the past twelve months what percentage of the talks you have been to were such that: (a) the technology failed (at some point); and/or (b) the slides were illegible for any normal-eyed person more than halfway back; and/or (c) if they could be read, they mostly couldn't be understood; and/or (d) the spoken and visual words bore little relationship to each other; and/or (e) the slide text was read, verbatim and boringly ("Do you think I can't read?"); and/or (f) the talk was going on too long and some interesting-looking slides were jettisoned, apparently at random, because of lack of time?

*The worst aspect of PowerPoint is the boring thing – but then they do at least turn off the lights so you can go to sleep!*

At the serious risk of our being over-prescriptive, the '6P Rule' may be helpful here: "Planning and Preparation Prevent Pitifully Poor Performance". This might include the potential for dry-run and feedback sessions with your harshest and most trustworthy critics.

C: MANAGING THE PEOPLE

**At the end of the day...** So, highlighting again the importance of this whole topic...

*You have to have the ability to communicate effectively. The skill can be tuned (for improvement) but if you don't have it, things get very difficult.*

Communication 'cubed' is a leadership imperative – communication before, communication during, communication after.

## 10. Giving CREDIT

"I can live for a month on a good compliment." Mark Twain (1835–1910)

Our colleagues – up, down and sideways – need to be recognised and celebrated when they've done something good, or done something well. And your job, as a leader, is to do the recognising and celebrating, in the right context and in the right way.

In terms of bringing out the best in your people, recognising contributions and giving praise and credit where it is due is one of the most powerful – and most regularly underused – of motivators. However, this must be done carefully, and well, since it can be a possible source of resentment if it is done badly, or not at all.

*You need to be able to tell people honestly where they've done well. And don't give false praise. People recognise a 'snow job' in a microsecond.*

*Make sure your 'praising' or 'special thank you' letters don't sound like variations on a form letter with a few words made specific to the recipient. Your cats pick this kind of thing up very quickly, and their opinion of you will drop as a result.*

*Don't wait too long to give praise. Don't think "I'll tell her later" or "I'll chat to him when the project's over". Deferred praise doesn't cut it like instant recognition does – and you might even forget. If someone does a good job, tell them now.*

Awards and recognition can also be important drivers of change, and reinforce the behaviour you're seeking, for example in nurturing cross-boundary interaction or better teamwork, as well as just individual achievement.

But there is an important paradox here. Former US President Harry Truman once famously – and accurately – remarked: "It is amazing what you can accomplish if you do not care who gets the credit."

However, this is a paradox because it might lead to the conclusion that assigning credit 'ownership' is unimportant. Thus, while President Truman may well have been addressing the negative consequences of jostling for credit, it is, of course, through allocated (and peer-recognised) credit that we can motivate and encourage people, secure funding, get promoted, enhance peer credibility, etc., etc. To us, however, the important issues are the giving of credit, and ensuring that credit is not wrongly attributed. Taking the credit is not the prerogative of the leader.

> "No man will make a great leader who wants to do it all himself or get all the credit for doing it." Andrew Carnegie (1835–1919)

By the way, if you think you'll get much in the way of thanks or praise for what you have done as a leader, forget it. Most cats don't work that way. The Chinese maxim around leadership applies: "When the job gets done, the people say 'We did it ourselves'."

*When someone passes off your ideas as theirs, don't worry – you've won.*

**The personal touch...** Somehow, in the hurly burly busy-ness of our daily lives, we often forget to acknowledge and celebrate the very many special things that happen all around us – at home, at work or in the supermarket. But when we get it right it can have tremendous impact:

*More than twenty years back I can still remember my boss at the time saying: "I just can't tell you how proud I am of you." A simple bit of praise, delivered with real sincerity – and showing a deep belief in me, taking me to a new level of confidence in what I could achieve – has lasted me half a working lifetime!*

...and the personal handwritten note, or email, can mean a lot...

*Joe was a great contributor... World class, in fact. And a loyal supporter through some tough changes. Long in the tooth but short on appropriate airs and graces. One day I popped by his office for a chat. To my considerable surprise, centrepiece of his pinboard was a note I had dropped him six months previously. It went along the lines of "Great job, Joe. We're proud of you. Keep up the fantastic work."*

*What sometimes may seem not very important to you can very often have much greater significance to those on the receiving end.*

**Public recognition...** In the 'cats' environment, never underestimate the power of an award to indicate appreciation and to motivate. From 'Best Client Relations Manager of the Month' to 'Most Informative Report' to 'Innovation of the Year'...

*...when it comes to recognition and awards, it's also good to make them visible, and make a fuss. And generally it's more about emotion, not about money. Acknowledgement by peers is a big deal.*

*Public recognition and praise for the contribution played by many people in achieving beneficial outcomes for the organisation... brings out the very best in people.*

But a word of caution – if you're going to be acknowledging quite a long list of people, make really sure – by double checking – that you don't miss any key contributors from that list. Elementary, you may think, but when this happens it is probably worse than giving no recognition at all.

> *In a group email, celebrating achievement, it is usually a mistake to single out just two or three individuals. The other 47 say to themselves "What about me? I work hard too!" The individual note works wonders.*

**Formal acknowledgement and attribution...** When in doubt, err on the side of generosity in acknowledging the contributions of others in published material. There's no downside. Everyone usually knows who the key contributors are.

In a 'cats' environment there are not many areas where you – as a leader – need to be neurotic, and go obsessively into the detail, but acknowledging others' contributions is one, especially where text is used verbatim. When it comes to reports or publications, for instance, omitting a key contributor's name, whether unintentionally or even if merely in error, generally has long-term negative consequences. So be warned.

### And continue to stretch...

> *There's no doubt that encouragement and persuasion work well (in bringing out the best in your people). But people don't just need praise, sometimes they need to know that you believe that they haven't done quite as well as you think they can do.*

**Claiming (all the) credit, and worse... There is a final point here:**

> *Selfishness in not sharing credit can bring out the worst in people.*

Further, claiming credit where it is not due is the kiss of death to the credibility of a leader:

> *Thirty years' back our department head sought to muscle his name in on our work (unsuccessfully I might add, but not without some heated – and at that stage potentially career-limiting – exchanges). Even after his funeral it was a historical act of inappropriateness that still sprung to mind when his name came up. And worse – I nearly slipped into the temptation myself decades later, sheepishly apologising in horror when I realised what I was doing.*

## MANAGING THE PEOPLE – In Conclusion

We keep returning, like a mantra, to the principle:

*All business is people business.*

In a 'cats' environment you need to be collegiate, not commanding. And in truth the ONLY long-term, sustainable advantage for you and your organisation lies with your talented people. Handle them with thought and care – and as a priority. Pursue excellence where enthusiasm and judgement also exist – the three go hand in hand. Interrogate track record unashamedly. Note that difficult people abound; perversely they are often the creative lifeblood of your operation.

> *More than eighty per cent of your success will depend on your ability to pick people – getting others, whom you trust, to offer differing perspectives is usually valuable. And continue to look carefully at those who are already with you. 'New brooms' can take a lot of your time, and are not always successful.*

Provide the shoulders for others to climb on – developing your star talent is too frequently neglected. You will also need to put in hard work to build your team – remember: 'Together Everyone Achieves More'.

Be clear about performance expectations and work to improve your skills in giving feedback. But when a situation is problematic, trust your gut feeling (and experience) and don't waste too much time. More dangerously, don't duck the issue and hope the problem will go away. Help people who need to be moved on to do so, with compassion.

As a 'conductor', your leadership baton is communication excellence. All too often, communication is badly done – the root of many (probably most?) day-to-day problems in organisations. Make sure that you and your 'orchestra' are reading from the same score – and remember that it is up to you to read theirs, not vice versa. The wording you choose to use, verbally or in writing, is critical and will usually be closely scrutinised. And, of course, it's way beyond just the words; behaviour, body language etc. all tell a story – and can show your support and approval very clearly. Communication is especially important in an environment of change – the reason why we choose to emphasise 'communication cubed'. You can never do enough.

Lastly – and certainly not least – harness the too-often much neglected motivational power of saying "thank you" and/or "well done", timeously and generously. A sincere, personal touch in celebration or praise giving – whether through the informal hand-written note or phone call, or appropriate 'hoopla' of well-deserved awards – is often remembered long after its origins are forgotten.

Once again, we can't emphasise enough that all business is people business.

## D: LEADING STRATEGICALLY

Much is talked about 'strategy'. Voluminous tomes abound. The same is true of 'change'.

So, last, but very much not least, in this small 'guidebook' we have sought to address the essence – and interrelationships – of strategy and change, and the ways in which we see them as applicable to the 'business' of herding professional cats.

We address the need to have goals that are stretching and inspiring – yet ultimately achievable. And for making the tough choices, and focusing effort predominantly on these goals. Strategic planning, in a nutshell, features. As does the priority for straightforward – and repetitive – communication.

Effective change is what good leaders do, indeed what they mostly do. Succeeding in the complex, conservative, often Machiavellian world of the professions is hard, fraught with sophisticated opposition, and with risk – both personal and organisational.

We provide you with some pointers that we have found useful.

### 11. Strategy is about CHOICE

> "The leader's role is to describe reality, and give hope."
> Napoleon Bonaparte (1769–1821)

In other words…

> *You need to tell a realistic story about where we are, and an optimistic story of where we're headed.*

Remembering…

> *Strategy is never meaningful unless it results in a reallocation of resources.*

**Rolling back from the future...** Canada's Wayne Gretsky was, by all accounts, the greatest ever ice hockey player. In a tough, bruising, competitive sport he also earned the trophy, five times, for being "the most gentlemanly player". He has been cited as among the top ten greatest athletes of the twentieth century. Carrying his fans' mantle of 'The Great One' with tact and humility, he was once asked, "Why are you so good?" His reply (bear in mind that ice hockey is played with a thing called a puck) was along the lines of: "I guess that in hockey, as in life, I've always tried to focus on where the puck's gonna be, not where it is now." And that's where he skated with great effect.

This provides in a few words the essence of good strategy – rolling backwards from the future, not extrapolating forwards from the present.

**Big goals...**

*It's vital to be able to describe and sell the future in an inspirational way.*

Creating a strategic vision requires thinking on a different scale from the day-to-day requirements of leading and managing. Your strategy must not be just a variation on the status quo. It should seek to take the organisation to a different, higher, level of performance, and stature. It should seek to galvanise and inspire:

*In our profession – highly competitive for talent as it is – you need to make sure you give your direct reports, or your team, a really major challenge.*

*It's so easy to get lost in the small things. But so important – and hard – to make the big bets.*

More than five hundred years ago Michelangelo said "The greater danger for most of us lies not in setting our aim too high and falling short, but in setting our aim too low, and achieving our mark." In the same vein, author Jim Collins in his book *Built to Last* talks about the importance of 'B.H.A.G.S.' (verbalised as 'bee-hags') – Big Hairy Audacious Goals. Even St Francis had a relevant prayer... "Protect us, O Lord, when our dreams are too little."

> *We had a big game plan – to raise our ambitions, and explore uncharted territories.*
>
> *Trusting in our big ideas is a priority for us, and people know it.*
>
> *If I could go back twenty years, I'd be even more ambitious.*
>
> *When it comes to employing talented people, the good news is that we're in Silicon Valley. But it's only good news if you're working on something big and important – otherwise the most talented people won't work with you; they'll go elsewhere.*

A small cautionary note, however, since there should be limits to 'bigness'. Intelligent people will realise immediately if your goal is completely unachievable in the timescales you've set. Thereafter, you're into 'mission impossible' territory:

> *Leadership is all about credibility. You can set any stretch target and have some ideas on how to meet it, but if you set it out too far the credibility with the team is essentially zero. Equally, if you set a target which is only a marginal improvement on where you are, the inspiration to move and do things differently is again zero. It's like the old rubber band analogy: you stretch it too tight and credibility is broken; you have it too slack and there's no drive for change.*

**Focus, focus, focus...** Most importantly, of the plethora of possibilities and options that will commonly open up for you, a 'focus on the few' is essential.

> "It is our choices, Harry, that show who we truly are, far more than our abilities." Albus Dumbledore, Headmaster, Hogwarts School of Witchcraft in *Harry Potter and the Chamber of Secrets*. JK Rowling (1965– )

Reflecting on, and sharing what got him involved with – and, more importantly, excited by – the possibility of a career in science, Dr Ramesh Mashelkar tells another – wonderful – story. As a small boy, he was fortunate in having a teacher who was passionate about science. One day, this man took the junior physics class out into the hot Indian sun to talk about optics, measuring the focal length of lenses – you may remember the exercise: varying the distance between the lens and a piece of paper, concentrating the sun's rays to a spot. As the paper blackened and smoke formed, and with the first lick of a flame, Ramesh's teacher turned to him, and looked into his eyes – looked into his soul as Ramesh describes it – and said: "See, Ramesh, look what happens when you focus your energy – you can set the world on fire. Indeed, you can set the world on fire."

> *Strategy is about choice. It's saying we're going to focus on these things, and not on those. This is where we are going to put our effort.*

**Planning strategically...** Once it has been decided that a new strategy is needed, the evolution of that strategy requires unwavering commitment. It cannot be done effectively when just squashed into the spaces of the day job. While it is unrealistic to expect the leader to drop everything to concentrate solely on strategy, he or she needs someone at their elbow who is single-mindedly devoted to working with them to keep the process of strategy formulation in the forefront of activity.

So the strategic planning process itself necessarily has a beginning, a middle and an end, all of which have differing requirements.

> *In a professional services business, strategy is about differentiation. Your partners want to know what your firm can do that others can't. So you have to define that.*

The start of the planning process requires a careful appraisal of the current position. Before you can decide where to go, it is necessary to know where you are. This requires definition of the so-called current realities:

*Change starts with a frank and transparent assessment of where we are, warts and all.*

However, the development of a strategy also needs to be preceded by the determination, or re-examination, of your mission and vision statements. These provide the contexts in which strategy can evolve and a strategic plan be formulated for achieving the goals that are identified, and sought. Furthermore, there should be an analysis of the broader landscape in which your strategic action is to be pursued.

*Describing your current environment – technical and business – is the first priority in strategic planning. And people make assumptions, which you need to examine closely. This should be a fact-based procedure.*

This part of the process will need to be followed by the planning exercise itself, which usually requires bringing together groups of staff with different responsibilities and rankings within your organisation. The overall process is generally a formidable one, so it will usually be best – and at a comparatively early stage – to seek to narrow the range of alternatives quite significantly. Decisions are not irreversible, and alternatives that were initially discarded can always be revived at a later stage. In all cases, however, there will be a need to achieve a good balance between 'top down' planning, usually led strongly by the more senior officers, and 'bottom up' planning which allows the general cohort of staff, on whom the success of implementation will be strongly dependent, to make meaningful inputs and to feel ownership.

*The skills and insights of those at the frontline are extremely valuable – and regularly and systematically disregarded by the policy makers at the top.*

Stanford Professor of Management, Robert Burgelman, talks about the importance of tapping into the 'wisdom of the ant hill'. In this vein, some while back, one of us was working in an environment of intense change. The organisation was getting some good help with strategy from external consultants. Six weeks into the project someone asked: 'I wonder what the people think?' Lots of well-organised, energised, time-bound task groups later, we found there was essentially a one-to-one correspondence with what the consultants had come up with. (They were, after all, listening hard and consolidating.) A lesson not to be forgotten.

> *Proclaiming messages from the top – without getting organisation ownership of decisions taken – will lead to scepticism.*

After these deliberations the plan needs to be wrapped up in a suitable package and then communicated widely and effectively – and repeatedly:

> *In terms of vision and strategic development… you can never tell the story enough times, either within the institution or externally.*

We believe it's worth reiterating a quote we used in Chapter 9:

> *You must, repeat must, keep your strategic messages very clear, and few in number; very straightforward, easily understood and digestible. Simple terms, easy to remember and to understand, and to pass on. And then repeat, repeat, repeat – be boring!*

**For the desk of the 'One Minute Leader'…**

**A quick summary around planning strategically:**

**Step 1:** Make a realistic – and as far as possible quantitative – assessment of your current broad environment (institution, system, country, world), and envisaged (e.g. ten-year) shifts. SWOT (Strengths/Weaknesses/Opportunities/Threats) and

PEST (Political/Economic/Social/Technological) analyses can help.

**Step 2:** Strategic intent – where do you want to be? (Recognising good strategy is not rolling forward from the present, but rolling back from the future.)

**Step 3:** How do you get from A to B? (Choices, and prioritisation). Articulate the set of tasks and tactics, and follow through. And then, in parallel...

**...Step 4:** Communicate, communicate, communicate – simply, and repetitively.

> *Over thirty years of practising it, I've learned three things about strategy. One: Less is more – drop things, and prioritise. Two: 'stay the course' – change is hard and takes time. Three: 'simplify' – plain English, repetitively, and simple models.*

> *Since taking over two years back I only talk about three things: delivering good outcomes, trusting our big ideas, and the importance of first-class talent.*

**Outside help, and the external perspective...** There are very mixed views about the extent to which 'outside' help and advice should be a part of enabling the strategic planning process.

In the first instance, the external perspective – for example what top 'competitors' are doing – can provide useful insights; 'keeping up with (or ahead of?) the Joneses' can prove helpful both in getting nay-sayers on board, and in strengthening the resolve of your supporters – and providing them with some ammunition:

> *Getting some top consultants to spend time with us, helping us identify weaknesses and problem areas, was really valuable. These messages were reinforced when, not inexpensively, we took the whole leadership team 'on tour', exposing them, in a*

> *concentrated fashion, to what top 'sister' organisations were doing. The lights came on, and stayed on.*

But, when it comes to employing the consultancy profession, in the world of (other) professionals, consultants are often treated with a mixture of scepticism and suspicion:

> *Forget the old 'borrowing your watch to tell you the time' adage. These guys came in, started a fire and then got paid for putting it out!*

> *When I think about the use of consultants, I am reminded that I often found our people don't value it if someone else tells them – they should discover it themselves.*

But there is a counter view…

> *I found the use of consultants valuable in giving messages that I knew in my bones were the right ones, but needed the 'prophet from without' to articulate them.*

> *The Board were much more on side with the proposed changes with the big name consultants' thick report and PowerPoint presentations behind them.*

And further: the fresh eye from the outsider can often help you 'distinguish the wood from the trees' – those 'big picture' things that get missed in the rough-and-tumble of working life. Similarly:

> *After working with the consultants, we realised we were probably moving into 'boiled frog' country: you know the old story – the frog in water that warms up gradually never jumps out, and dies. The frog who jumps into hot water, jumps out. They helped us see where the water was getting really hot.*

Thus, correctly managed – repeat, correctly managed – our view is that the external perspective can add a lot of value. This can be leveraged if and when you have your own talented staff working closely with the external players – with a designated responsibility to oversee the implementation stages after the consulting assignment has formally concluded. Taking real ownership is very important in ensuring that the insights you might get from external help in crafting good strategy get properly calibrated and embedded in your organisation...

*I see elegant strategies – developed, for example, by the very bright people the consultants brought in – falter when it comes to getting them applied in practice. The brilliant analysts who crunch the data and imagine new futures have rarely, if ever, persuaded a shop steward to accept substantial changes in job descriptions or job losses. They have never had to deal with the arrogance of surgeons who always know best, or the scarred bureaucrats whose occasional experiences of moving beyond the comfort of prescribed rules and procedures have left them battered and bruised.*

Further, and finally, seek to get the maximum 'bang for your buck' when harnessing external advice in the professional environment, where there are often severe budgetary constraints. There can be problems with employing the 'heavyweights' from the ranks of the consultants, not least because of the expense involved. It is great to chat with the senior partner(s) doing the pitch, but (frequently) disappointing when the two-year-in juniors, working 100-hour weeks, end up doing the job. The smaller, more specialised, and usually less expensive, 'boutique' providers often have a mind of their own and an ability to be creatively objective. Here, what you see is very much what you get.

**Managing risk...** While strategy is about aspiration and intent, there is, of course, a place for formally identifying – and examining – the major risks your institution might face. That is just good leadership practice. But nowadays it seems that a whole industry has arisen around risk assessment, key threats, and the like. It has led, sadly and far too often, to a tendency for 'box ticking':

*You can spend an awful lot of time imagining – and documenting – the worst that can happen. It's bananas!*

> *Very often you just have to manage the things that arise, as best you can.*
>
> *Most of the nuts and bolts stuff around risk we did (just) for the benefit of the Risk Committee.*
>
> *You need to apply healthy common sense. And not slavishly obey the professional advice you get given. And understand, for example, especially with your lawyers and contract people, where they are coming from, which is often a position of total risk aversion.*
>
> *Every leadership job will have crises. And typically not the crises that you can anticipate. They just fall out of the sky.*

But forewarned, forearmed: and some thoughtful reflection around the risks you might encounter on your strategic journey can be a positive aid to your strategic planning. As a senior business executive once remarked to us, far from arrogantly, about the very well-known firm he worked for "The future will never surprise us – we've already been there." Thus:

> *One can be too dismissive of risk management. It can of course be (and often is) a box-ticking exercise. But it doesn't have to be. At its best it can be a positively-structured way of understanding the strengths and weaknesses of strategy.*

## 12. Leading and managing CHANGE

> "Even if you are on the right track you will get run over if you just sit there." Will Rogers (1879–1935)

Whether it's based on strategic thinking or simply arises as a result of external circumstance, change is ever present and inevitable in professional domains.

Change must be led and must be managed:

> *Leadership implies change. Good leaders take what is not working, or not working well, and change it so that it works better.*

> *Powerful speeches and fine rhetoric don't (often) change culture – you need structure and process to deliver culture change, and embed it.*

Robust thought and dialogue – the bread and butter of professional life – is often a major prerequisite for important change in our world. But just try to get the average member of your staff even to shift offices...

> *Change is great so long as someone else is changing.*

> *Bringing about change can be a tricky exercise. The ability to ignore and push back is immense.*

### And change is hard...

> *The analysis and high-level decisions behind strategy never fully account for the blood, sweat and toil in getting change implemented and getting people to do things.*

> *Even the best leaders have often been away from the coalface so long that they forget the realities of getting apprehensive and insecure people, tired and frightened of change, and deeply skeptical of the motivations (and competence) of senior management, to do things they're not used to. It is messy and difficult and often only partially successful. But it is leadership in action.*

**Resistance...** In any change initiative, one of the most difficult tasks is getting 'buy in', and trying to promulgate a sense of ownership of the necessity for change:

> *After a thirty-year career in the organisation, one of the most senior executives – at his farewell dinner – bemoaned how hard it was to embed new ways of doing things. "The people are like seaweed," he reflected, "Just keep your head down, they say, and it will all wash over you, as will the next wave."*

> *In an early meeting with some of my most distinguished and long-serving 'cats' the essence was: "Well, you seem*

> *like a pretty good guy, you may even be better than your predecessors, but in due course you will leave and we will still be here."* The feeling expressed was that new management is a temporary disturbance to the smooth running of the organisation.

> *We can be incredibly resistant to change… because of the focus on individual excellence and achievement – they're independent beings, and there's little collaboration. So you have to start early in people's careers, supporting and rewarding and promoting collaborative behaviour and team playing, building a sense of pride in the organisation as a whole. And we need to train the next generation differently, to go out there and be reformers.*

Niccolò Machiavelli was a great herder of cats. His comments are as relevant today as they were in 1532:

> "And it ought to be remembered that there is nothing more difficult to take in hand, more perilous to conduct, or more uncertain in its success, than to take the lead in the introduction of a new order of things. Because the innovator has for enemies all those who have done well under the old conditions, and lukewarm defenders in those who may do well under the new…"

And be warned: those enemies of change can get very energised, and well organised…

> *Whenever something happens, or is planned, or is only just being seriously talked about, the 'old boys' network' gets unleashed and I'll get thirty letters from around the country saying what a bad idea this is and how life as we know it will surely come to an end if it happens.*

**Listen carefully…** The reasons for change may be self-evident to you as the leader but this clarity, more often than not, does not penetrate far down into your organisation. Thus, before change is initiated, a period of careful and sensitive listening should be the rule not the exception:

*I first ask "What do we want to change, and why?" Then I urge a new leader to consult, consult, consult; listen and learn before acting on the change you want to enact.*

*In the first three months of a new job you mostly need to be listening, across all levels in your organisation. You need to make sure you're familiar with your environment before embarking on change.*

*Consultation is the basis for all good decisions and, therefore, open your door to all the stakeholders in these decisions.*

*I took on a top job on 1 March. On 2 March I contacted the senior 250 people across the organisation with just four questions. One, what are the three most important things we should be doing? Two, what are our most important challenges and opportunities? Three, how can we strengthen our linkages across the organisation? Four, how do we retain, develop and recruit the best talent? I later opened this up to all the staff, and we got some great feedback and ideas.*

**Think carefully...** Change consumes a lot of energy. Like the old marriage service used to remind us – as we said previously – it is not to be taken on "lightly, wantonly or unadvisedly". It is, therefore, important to identify, and separate out, those parts that aren't broken and don't need radical changing from those that are, and do. As Lucius Cary, Lord Falkland, said in 1641 (this quote is often attributed to John F. Kennedy): "When it is not necessary to change, it is necessary not to change."

*For the things that aren't broken, but can still be improved, you don't need to turn the whole organisation on its head.*

*Next time around I definitely wouldn't embark on changing so many things at the same time. I'd plan better and take more consideration of individuals' capacity to absorb and cope.*

*We need to be aware that change is really threatening for many people. So you need to address the 'soft' issues of*

> *feelings and anxiety as much as the 'hard' issues of resources and the implementation timetable.*

**Beware the 'big bang'...** Although it can be tempting, and sometimes advantageous, to bring about change as quickly as possible – and all at once, to 'get it over with' – this can have unintended, negative consequences. Erring on the side of caution can have beneficial effects both in embedding the changes and in making them more palatable to those affected.

Evidently the seafaring explorers of old, prior to setting out on a voyage into the unknown (not a bad metaphor for some change programmes!), used first to 'port-hop' along more familiar coastlines to test things out – their ship, their tools, and their team:

> *Piloting was very important. We took the feedback, refined the approach and then rolled the changes out through the organisation.*

> "Before anything else, preparation is the key to success." Alexander Graham Bell (1847–1922)

On the other hand, being too cautious brings with it the dangers of paralysis by analysis – 'fiddling while Rome burns', so to speak. People do need to sense urgency. Also, perceptions that consultation is going to be 'continuous' allows well-organised rearguard actions to be set up, aimed at preserving the status quo. Therefore...

> *Once the way forward is clear, be decisive. People generally want to feel positive about their work – give them the opportunity to do so by making the tough decisions quickly.*

Here we have another paradox which requires experience and judgement if it is to be overcome effectively:

> *When I started, I was given two pieces of advice by some senior players in my business world. One group said that it was essential that that I make all the major changes in*

> *my first year, as after that nothing much would happen. Another group told me, with equal belief, that I should not rush into change and, whatever I did, not to change too much in Year 1. I made up my own mind.*

**Anticipation...** In some cases the change that you are seeking to bring about will also have been foreseen by (at least) the more perceptive of your colleagues, and enlisting them to facilitate the process can have advantages:

> *As Darwin said, it is not the strongest of the species that survives, nor the most intelligent; it is the one that is most adaptable to change. Going further than Darwin, I think it's fair to say that only those who can anticipate the change can lead the change.*

> "Look for intelligence and judgment and, most critically, a capacity to anticipate, to see around corners." General Colin Powell (1937– )

**Support for change...** When you get seriously engaged in taking change forward it can be valuable to have a 'lead agent', engaged totally and full-time in leading and facilitating the change process.

That said:

> *If you appoint a radical agent for change you must also ensure that there is elbow room for them to bring the change about. Support from above is essential, and a sufficient level of support to ensure that people know it's serious.*

Equally, however, if the change agent (who may well be you) does not have real and visible support from above, then you will largely be wasting your time. Find a new passion, or a new organisation.

**Communication clarity...**

> *In times of difficulty or change, a lack of frequent and straightforward communication about either the challenges*

> *facing an organisation or the roadmap for change breeds uncertainty. Uncertainty of this nature destroys focus, productivity and commitment.*

The reasons for introducing changes need to be very evident, particularly to senior leadership, but also at grassroots level. Further, you need to be crystal clear about where you're headed. The key task of leadership (along with a positive and constructive mindset) is to articulate and communicate clearly, using simple, straightforward, easy-to-remember – and few – messages.

> *Change is spelt: communicate, communicate, communicate.*

> *Get the language right. If you present in a way they don't understand, there are dangers. Especially beware 'management speak'.*

> *Once, in building the case for change, I made a blunder by quoting management guru Tom Peters' "If it ain't broke, break it" – talking about the need to 'reinvent' one's own business regularly in order to stay alive in an intensely competitive, commercial environment. This went down like a lead balloon in our place.*

An important part of the message is also to build, as positively as you can, on the past.

> *You need to recognise the place from whence they've come, and acknowledge what has been achieved. Just because change is now needed, doesn't mean they failed personally.*

**Your (only?) tool for driving change...** The use of developmental resources, in money or kind, can be a valuable way of enhancing the prospect of successful change, at the right pace and in the right way. It is profitable to remember the Golden Rule:

> *He who has the gold makes the rules.*

In practice, this usually means...

*Your most important – and perhaps your only – tool for change is creative, temporary cross-transfer of resources (both financial and personnel). Both adjectives are essential. This is a radically non-heroic proposition, but it works.*

*Put out the cream, and they'll come.*

Managing – and especially managing change – is a long-haul trip. As such, in 'sticking to the game plan', managing for continuity and succession should be in the job plan for at least the 'second hundred days' of the senior change leader. Regrettably, most often it isn't.

**In summary...** One of the best (and simplest) articulations of effective change management we have encountered comes from Oren Harari of the Graduate School of Business at the University of San Francisco. In his book *Leapfrogging the Organisation* he advocates 'U2D2' guidance. First – and in the context of the organisation's history, the prevailing culture and your external environment – ensure that there is a clear and widespread Understanding of the need for change. Secondly, that there is clarity about the Direction in which you're headed. Thirdly, that it always takes longer than you think, and people can get deflected or bored – therefore keep the Urgency button on. And finally – day in, day out, month in, month out – the Discipline of ensuring well-planned execution excellence, with clear accountabilities and delivery on the action steps agreed.

## LEADING STRATEGICALLY – In Conclusion

Strategy should get you from where you are now to where you want to be. Both of these positions need to be clearly articulated – your 'current reality' and your (hopefully) inspiring 'vision' of the future. Choices need to be made between the possible alternative futures, and you will have to prioritise the actions you need to take in moving you from your inherited present to your envisaged future.

Aim high, but ensure that your targets have achievability, and you will get (good) stretch from your people. Indeed your people, correctly engaged, can also be a great source of wisdom in contributing to defining the future that you – and, with luck, they – wish to create. Listen to them.

Too much attention (or paranoia) around 'risk' can engender aversion and a lowering of your sights and, in turn, a loss of energy and enthusiasm.

Nothing will happen, however, unless resources (money and time) are allocated – or reallocated – to your strategic priorities. And little will happen if you don't pay sufficient attention to ensuring clear and widespread understanding of your chosen direction, and the reasons for it – laid out in clear, concise and straightforward terms, and reinforced repetitively, and over the long haul.

Inevitably, your strategy will lead to change, indeed it may well itself be transformational in spirit. But change is hard work and requires careful forethought, detailed planning and – if you can – piloted implementation.

As we have said, 'communication cubed' – communication before, communication during and communication after – is a prerequisite for success.

## POSTSCRIPT – A CLOSING THOUGHT

Finally, the essence of leading strategically and managing effectively in a 'cats' environment was aptly summarised by one of our colleagues:

*I reckon there are five key dimensions to leadership in a professional environment…*
*1. As a leader, you must have a vision of where you want the organisation to go – because if you don't, no one else will.*
*2. You articulate it, and communicate it well, to get your people excited.*
*3. You hire the best people you can find.*
*4. You create the environment where they can excel, and succeed.*
*5. You get out of the way.*

\* \* \* \*

And here are our suggestions (our 'twelve Cs'!) for your leadership '**Checklist**':

**Culture:** passionate, argumentative, political, often closely tied to organisational history and sometimes flavoured with bureaucracy. Embed progress (and 'change') into the history. Be a red-tape vigilante. Ask yourself if you're comfortable leading in this type of environment. If not, look elsewhere.

**Conflict:** the 'bread and butter' of the cats community, often trivial in nature (and in perceived consequence) but potentially incendiary in emotion. Handle with care, tact and time. There are ALWAYS (at least) two sides to every story.

**Collaboration:** impeded by tradition, performance metrics and many common organisational systems. But it is the future, and interfaces are 'where all the exciting innovations happen'.

Look for (personal) boundary crossing opportunities and promote effective 'collabronauts'.

**Charge (the taking of):** mobility rules – be 'out and about'. Credibility is your passport; and clear, well-communicated goals are your focus. With corresponding clarity – and shared understanding – around 'who's gotta do what by when' (roles and responsibilities). Manage your time, yourself and your stakeholders overtly. Trust your intuition, but prepare thoughtfully. Expect some failures, and take responsibility. Don't vacillate.

**Composure:** needed under pressure – which there will always be. Plan well, stick to your guns and obsess around effective implementation. Follow-up is essential, including around the detail.

**Committees:** necessarily what is needed to get quite a lot of things done, well or badly, but they are no substitute for managing through people. Ask: do you need one? Is the brief tight? Are the documents (inputs and outputs) concise? Have you got the best Chair you can find?

**Cash:** makes the world go around. Often your only tool for effecting change. There will ALWAYS never be enough. Make yourself financially literate, use skilled help and seek access to some 'discretionary dollars'.

**Colleagues:** don't think 'subordinates'. Talent management (with strategy) should top your job list. Seek out excellence, and enthusiastic spirits. Build trust (it takes TIME); quit when it is absent. Hone your juggling skills for the task/team/individual balancing act. Delegate (at double the level you first thought of) but with crystal clear accountabilities – with follow-up. Become excellent at giving feedback and managing performance. Beware divisions between line and support staff. All business is people business.

**Communication:** THE baton of leadership. Poor communication is ubiquitous. And (your) actions speak louder than words. Think through your email strategy (develop one if you don't already have one). Gain skills in being comfortable with the media, social and otherwise. Communicate before, communicate during, communicate after.

**Credit:** remember the important sentiment about 'living comfortably for a month on a good compliment'. The personal touch has real power and is often underutilised.

**Choice:** what 'strategy' is all about. This, not that. Rolling backwards from the future you have envisioned, not extrapolating forwards from the present you have inherited. And the need to articulate honestly. Think big, with stretch, but ultimately with achievability. Then focus your efforts. Focus, focus, focus. And it won't be a strategy unless resources shift.

**Change:** probably why you're doing this job – the status quo is unsatisfactory to you. Support may, especially at first, be lukewarm. Resistance will be determined, and probably well organised. Be very clear about the direction in which you're headed, and why. Communicate obsessively. Focus on the few, key 'strategic messages' – very simple, very clear and often repeated. Plan and manage tightly around execution. Act with urgency.

Once they've decided they like you, cats make good companions.

# ABOUT THE AUTHORS

**Graeme Davies** is Emeritus Vice-Chancellor of the University of London, a post he held from 2003 to 2010, following eight years as Principal of the University of Glasgow. He was Chief Executive of the Higher Education Funding Council for England from 1991 until 1995, after having been Vice-Chancellor of the University of Liverpool from 1986 to 1991. He was awarded a knighthood in the Queen's January 1996 Honours List for his services to higher education.

Sir Graeme is currently Chairman of the UK's Higher Education Policy Institute. He is also Chairman and President of the British University Vietnam in Hanoi. He is a Non-Executive member of the Public Interest Body of PriceWaterhouseCoopers LLP, London. He has held visiting professorships in New Zealand, Brazil, China, Argentina, South Africa, Israel and India.

Born in New Zealand, Graeme's tertiary education was with the School of Engineering of the University of Auckland where he studied aeronautical engineering, and gained a PhD in materials science – and was a university football blue. A materials engineer by subsequent training and practice, he has published widely, primarily in the fields of solidification and deformation, and is the author or co-author of seven books. He was Professor of Metallurgy and Head of Department at the University of Sheffield from 1977 to 1986, having taken up that post after sixteen years in the Department of Metallurgy and Materials Science at the University of Cambridge where he was also a Fellow of St Catharine's College.

Graeme is a Fellow of the Royal Academy of Engineering and a Fellow of the Royal Society of Edinburgh. He is also an Honorary Fellow of the Royal Society of New Zealand, and holds honorary degrees from thirteen universities.

He is married to English linguistics academic, Florence. They have two children, Michael and Helena, and four grandchildren. His interests include bird-watching, cricket and doing the *Times* crossword.

**Geoff Garrett** is Queensland Chief Scientist, having completed eight years as Chief Executive of Australia's Commonwealth Scientific and Industrial Research Organisation (CSIRO), one of the world's largest and most diverse national research organisations.

Prior to joining CSIRO, Geoff led South Africa's national science agency, the CSIR, as President and Chief Executive from 1995, following five years as Executive Vice President: Operations. He was named South Africa's 'Boss of the Year' in 1998, and 'Engineer of the Year' by the South African Society of Professional Engineers in 1999.

Educated in the United Kingdom, Geoff is a graduate of Cambridge University where he completed a doctorate in metallurgy, and laboured hard on the cricket field under his captain, Graeme Davies. He was also a university boxing blue. He then took up a lecturing position at the University of Cape Town, and, prior to joining the CSIR, was Professor and Head of Department at the University of the Witwatersrand in Johannesburg. He held visiting positions at Brown University (RI, USA), and at Oxford and Sheffield Universities. His research interests centred around the fracture and fatigue behaviour of engineering materials.

Geoff is a Fellow of the Australian Academy of Technological Sciences and Engineering, the Royal Society of South Africa and the Australian Institute of Company Directors, and served on the Prime Minister's Science, Engineering and Innovation Council in Australia for eight years. He is currently Chairman of ANZIC, the twenty-two member Australian–New Zealand Consortium of the International Ocean Discovery Program (IODP).

A recipient of the Centenary Medal for service to Australian society through science, Geoff was named by the Australian Financial Review as one of Australia's 2008 'True Leaders'. In June 2008 he was appointed as an Officer of the Order of Australia (AO) in the Queen's Birthday Honours list.

He is married to Janet, and they have four sons, Ben, Matt, David and Luke. His interests include fishing and tennis, and his two (so far!) grandsons, Liam and Aran.

# INDEX

## A
Alumni 103
Annual Report 113
Anticipation 135
Appointments. *See* Hiring (staff)
Authorship 118
Awards. *See* Credit

## B
Boundary crossing 33–38
Bureaucracy/bureaucrats 26–28

## C
Calm, keeping 60–61, 61
Car parking. *See* Parking
Cash. *See* Resources
Chairman 74
Change 104, 125
Change (management) 61, 130–137, 137
Clever people 24, 29, 52, 102
Collaboration 34–38, 38, 58
Committees 68–74, 74
Communication 104–115, 115, 135
Compassion 101, 120
Complexity 35, 51
Conflict 29–33, 33
Consultants 93, 127–128, 128
Consultation 54, 133
Core values 25
Creativity 37, 108
Credibility 40, 49, 60
Credit 115, 118–119
Culture 19, 22–28, 28, 38

## D
Decision making/taking 51–55, 55, 134
Delegation 49, 59
Details 65, 80
Disciplinary action. *See* Termination (of employment)
Disciplinary action 103
Diversity 90

## E
Email 110–111
Enthusiasm 40, 86
Equal opportunity 90
Ethics 75
Excellence 84–85, 85
Execution. *See* Implementation

## F
Failure 56, 101
Feedback 32, 67, 100, 105
Finances. *See* Resources
Firing. *See* Termination (of employment)
First impressions 40
Focus 51, 123
Funding. *See* Resources

## G
Gender issues. *See* Equal opportunity
Goals 56, 122
Governance 74

## H
Health and safety 95
Hiring (staff) 84–92
History, learning from 23

## I
Implementation 64
Incentives 96
Influence 23
Innovation 92
Inspiration 122

Integrity 57
Intuition 91
IT projects 62

**J**

Judgement 82, 91

**L**

Leadership development 94
Listening skills 80, 105, 132
Loneliness 58

**M**

Making choices 77, 87, 121
Measurement. *See* Metrics
Media 112
Meetings 72
Metrics 66
Minutes 72
Money. *See* Resources
Motivation 28, 83, 96

**N**

Negative feedback 32
Networking 58, 59

**O**

Objectives. *See* Goals
Opposition 30, 55
Out and about. *See* Walking about

**P**

Parking 29, 96
Patience 67
Peer pressure 30
People 48, 103
Performance management 66, 98
Persistence 75
Piloting 134
Planning 61–63, 114, 125, 133
Politics 25
Popularity 31
Power 59
PowerPoint (death by) 114

Precedent 30
Preparation 41
Presentations 114
Project management 62
Promotion 87

**Q**

Qualifications 89

**R**

Recognition. *See* Credit
Red tape 28, 38
Referees 85
Relationships 37, 44, 75, 89, 110
Remuneration 29, 97
Resistance 30, 131
Resources 36, 76–78, 136
Respect 53
Results 80
Reviews 73
Risk, management of 129
Role clarity 56
Rules 26
Rumours 37, 107

**S**

Self knowledge 56
Silos 38
Simplification 127
Social media 111
Stakeholders 45
Stories 106
Straight talking. *See* Talking straight
Strategic planning 124–127
Strategy 121–130
Stretch 89
Structure 64, 99
Support staff 95

**T**

Talent 82–83, 87, 94, 123
Talking straight 25

Team 34, 79, 93
Tenacity 60
Termination (of employment) 100
Thank you (saying). *See* Credit
Time management 43
Time (that it always takes) 67, 137
Titles 96
Track record 85, 91
Training. *See* Leadership development
Transparency 59
Trust 59, 74

## U

Understanding. *See* Communication
Urgency 137

## V

Values 25, 75

## W

Walking about 40, 58
Work-life balance 43–45

Lightning Source UK Ltd.
Milton Keynes UK
UKOW030624280613

212926UK00008B/32/P